Mathemagic Puzzles & Brain Drainers

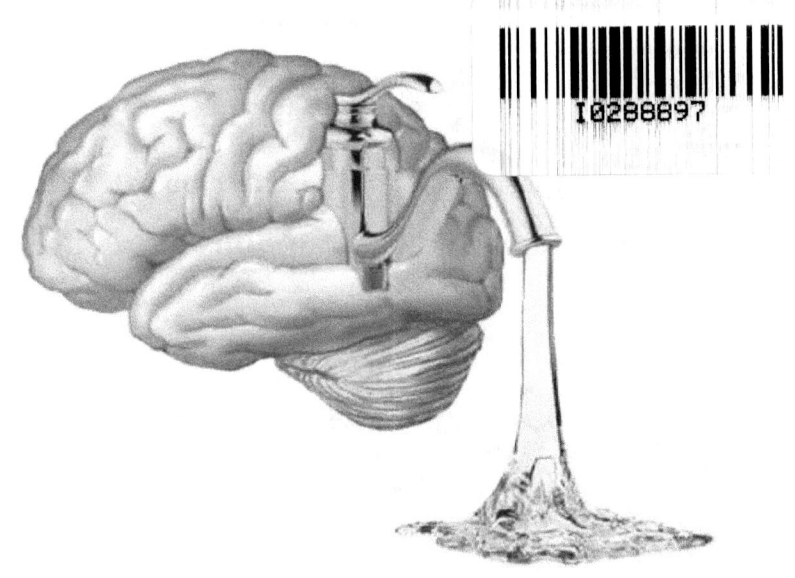

Published by:

F-2/16, Ansari Road, Daryaganj, New Delhi-110002
011-23240026, 011-23240027 • *Fax:* 011-23240028
Email: info@vspublishers.com • *Website:* www.vspublishers.com

Branch : Hyderabad
5-1-707/1, Brij Bhawan (Beside Central Bank of India Lane)
Bank Street, Koti, Hyderabad - 500 095
040-24737290
E-mail: vspublishershyd@gmail.com

Follow us on:

For any assistance sms **VSPUB** to **56161**
All books available at **www.vspublishers.com**

© Copyright: *V&S PUBLISHERS*
ISBN 978-93-815886-9-7
Edition 2013

The Copyright of this book, as well as all matter contained herein (including illustrations) rests with the Publishers. No person shall copy the name of the book, its title design, matter and illustrations in any form and in any language, totally or partially or in any distorted form. Anybody doing so shall face legal action and will be responsible for damages.

Printed at : Param Offsetters, Okhla, New Delhi-110020

Publisher's Note

After publishing a series of books on puzzles and quizzes, V&S Publishers has come out with this unique puzzle book on Mathematics, the *Mathemagic Puzzles & Brain Drainers*.

Since the year 2012 has been declared as the 'National Mathematical Year', this is definitely the ideal time to publish the book.

Mathemagic Puzzles & Brain Drainers contains different sections of **Puzzles, Brainteasers, Mind, Maths and Logic Quizzes, Brain Drainers, Math Riddles** and **Logic Games and Riddles.** In each of these sections, there are short, intelligent and interesting questions which will need a little exercise of your brains to solve them. The **Answers** to all the **Questions** have been given at the back of the book, section wise for your convenience.

The book is written in a simple, lucid and concise manner, and aims to develop and sharpen the logical, reasoning and mathematical skills of the readers, particularly the school and college going students.

The book contains brainteasing puzzles on simple principles of Mathematics like Algebra, Geometry, Arithmetic, Trigonometry, etc. to sharpen your logical and mathematical skills.

Hence, pick up the book as fast as you can and enjoy the fun of solving these mind-boggling math puzzles and riddles.

Contents

Questions

Puzzles to Puzzle You	6
Test Your Brain Power!	23
Brainteasers	24
Mind, Maths And Logic Quizzes	26
Brain Drainers	46
Math Riddles	52
Logic Games and Riddles	56

Answers

Puzzles	61
Brainteasers	77
Mind, Maths and Logic Quizzes	79
Brain Drainers	93
Math Riddles	97
Logic Games and Riddles	100

PUZZLES
TO
PUZZLE YOU

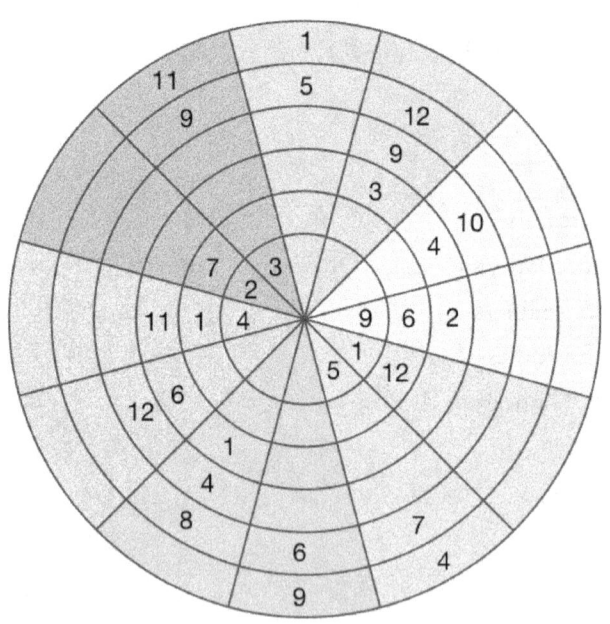

Puzzles

Puzzle 1

Mr Smith has lots of pound coins, ten boxes in all. Each box contains 100 pound coins, but one box contains coins which are all counterfeit and are slightly lighter, 1/16 of an ounce lighter to be exact.

The problem lies in the fact that they all look identical, the only way to tell them apart is to weigh them.

Mr Smith knows the correct weight for a box, but how many weighings are required to determine which box contains the counterfeit ones?

Puzzle 2

What number comes next in this sequence:

12 13 15 17 111 113 117 119 123 ==?==

Puzzle 3

You have the misfortune to own an unreliable clock. This one gains exactly 12 minutes every hour.

It is now showing 10pm and you know that is was correct at midnight, when you set it.

The clock stopped four hours ago, what is the correct time now?

Puzzle 4

The map below shows the street locations of a city. Position three police offi cers such that the entire length of every street can be seen by at least one offi cer.

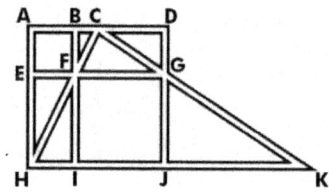

Puzzle 5

Can you determine which number best completes this puzzle?

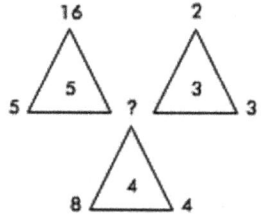

Puzzle 6

Using eight eights and addition only, can you make 1000?

8+8+8+8+8+8+8+8=1000

Puzzle 7

After visiting my Great Aunt Anne, I travelled home in her old jalopy. The car was old and battered, it had a leak from the petrol tank, and I was stuck in second gear.

This meant that I could only travel along at a steady 30 miles per hour and managed a paltry 20 miles per gallon of fuel.

At the start of the journey I had placed exactly 10 gallons of fuel into the tank. I knew though, that the fuel tank lost fuel at the rate of half a gallon per hour. Just as I arrived home, the car stopped because it had run out of fuel and I had only just made it.

How far was it from my Great Aunt's to my home?

Puzzle 8

Can you place the numbers 1 to 8 into the following grid. No two consecutive numbers can be directly next to each other either horizontally, vertically or diagonally.

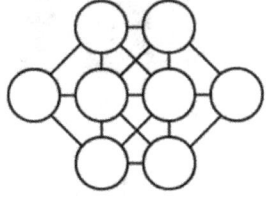

Puzzle 9

Starting in the bottom left corner and moving either up or right, one square at a time, adding up the numbers along the way, what

is the largest sum which can be made once you have reached the top right corner?

1	4	2	2	1	2
4	3	1	3	4	3
2	1	4	2	1	2
1	2	2	3	3	1
4	1	3	1	2	1
3	1	4	3	4	2
2	1	1	1	1	3
3	4	2	3	2	2

Puzzle 10

At the local model boat club, four friends were talking about their boats. There were a total of eight boats, two in each colour, red, green, blue and yellow. Each friend owned two boats. No friend had two boats of the same colour.

Alan didn't have a yellow boat. Brian didn't have a red boat, but did have a green one. One of the friends had a yellow boat and a blue boat and another friend had a green boat and a blue boat. Charles had a yellow boat. Darren had a blue boat, but didn't have a green one.

Can you work out which friend had which coloured boats?

Puzzle 11

A rope swing hangs vertically down so that the end is 12 inches from the ground, and 48 inches from the tree.

If the swing is pulled across so that it touches the tree, it is 20 inches from the ground.

How long is the rope?

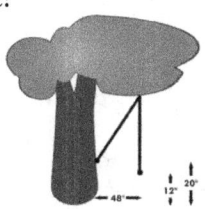

Puzzle 12

Three men are buried in the sand all facing forwards with their heads above ground.

Each man has a hat placed on his head selected from a bag containing 3 red hats, and 2 black hats, and the men knew the possible hat choices.

The men cannot turn around to see the men behind them.

The man at the back is asked what hat he is wearing. He replies, "I do not know". The middle man is asked what hat he is wearing. He also replies, "I do not know". The man at the front is then asked what hat he is wearing. He replies, "I am wearing a red hat".

How did he know?

Puzzle 13

Michael made a cake, in the shape of a perfect cube, for 64 guests at a recent party. The inside of the cake was sponge, and he iced the cake with red icing. He of course did not ice the bottom of the cake.

Michael cut each side of the cake into four equal pieces, making a total of 64 pieces of cake, each exactly the same size.

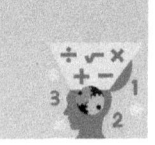

How many of the pieces of cake had at least 2 of their sides with icing?

Puzzle 14

Three people check into a hotel. They pay £30 to the manager and go to their room. The manager suddenly remembers that the room rate is £25 and gives £5 to the bellboy to return to the people. On the way to the room, the bellboy reasons that £5 would be diffi cult to share among three people, so he pockets £2 and gives £1 to each person. Now each person paid £10 and got back £1. So they paid £9 each, totalling £27. The bellboy has £2, totalling £29. Where is the missing £1?

Puzzle 15

How many squares, of any size, can you fi nd on this chessboard which do not contain a Rook?

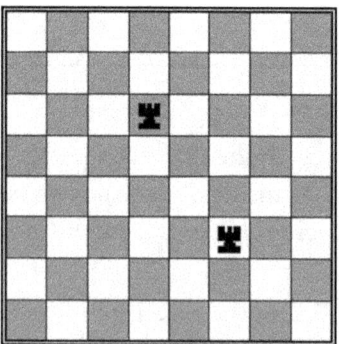

Puzzle 16

I have a machine which has four cogwheels in constant mesh. The largest cog has 168 teeth and the others have 49, 32 and 15 respectively. How many revolutions must the largest cog make before each of the cogs is back in its starting position?

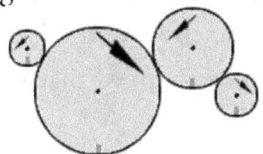

Puzzle 17

Starting with the 6 in the bottom left corner, what is the highest total you can make, if you only move up or right, using the mathematical signs on the way?

+	4	-	1	+	3
2	+	4	-	1	+
-	3	+	2	-	2
2	-	4	+	3	-
+	3	-	1	+	2
6	+	1	-	2	+

Puzzle 18

Place the digits 1 to 8 into the grid. The numbers you can see are the totals for the surrounding numbers.

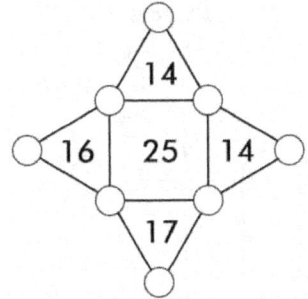

Puzzle 19

A woman had three old coins – a silver dollar, a quarter and a dime. Each coin was a little battered and had a piece missing. She found that exactly the same fraction had broken away from each coin.

What fraction of each was missing if the value of the remaining bits of coins was now exactly one dollar in total?

For this puzzle, it can be assumed that ½ of a coin is worth ½ of its value.

Puzzle 20

Can you fill the thermometers with mercury, such that the numbers outside the grid indicate how many cells in each row and column contain mercury.

Mercury always starts filling from the bottom of a thermometer and not every thermometer has to contain mercury.

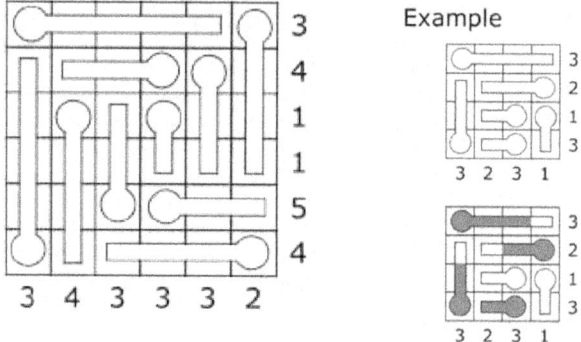

Puzzle 21

Using the digits 1 to 9, create three 3-digit numbers. The second number is twice the first. The third number is three times the first.

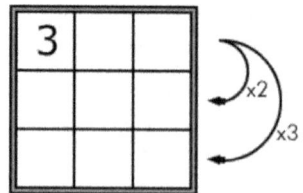

Puzzle 22

In the illustration, we have a sketch of Sir Edwyn de Tudor going to rescue his ladylove, the fair Isabella, who was held a captive by a neighbouring wicked baron. Sir Edwyn calculated that if he rode fifteen miles an hour, he would arrive at the castle an hour too soon, while if he rode ten miles an hour, he would get there just an hour too late. Now, it was of the first importance that he should arrive at the exact time appointed, in order that the rescue that he had planned should be a success, and the time of the tryst was five o'clock, when the captive lady would be taking her afternoon tea. The puzzle is to discover exactly how far Sir Edwyn de Tudor had to ride.

Puzzle 23

What value of * makes the following correct:

$$\frac{*}{*} - \frac{*}{2} + \frac{*}{4} = \frac{*}{12}$$

Puzzle 24

Complete the fifth circle with the correct dots.

   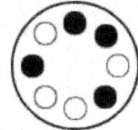 

Puzzle 25

Which square, which circle, and which triangle has the closest area to the doughnut shape on the left? The drawings are to scale, so you might be able to judge it, as well as working the actual areas out.

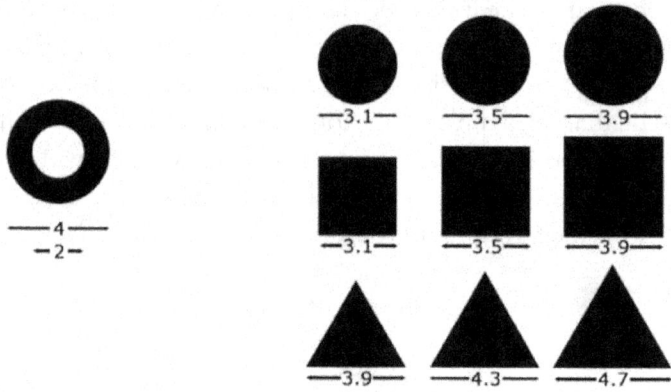

Puzzle 26

Can you fill the thermometers with mercury, such that the numbers outside the grid indicate how many cells in each row and column contain mercury.

Mercury always starts filling from the bottom of a thermometer and not every thermometer has to contain mercury.

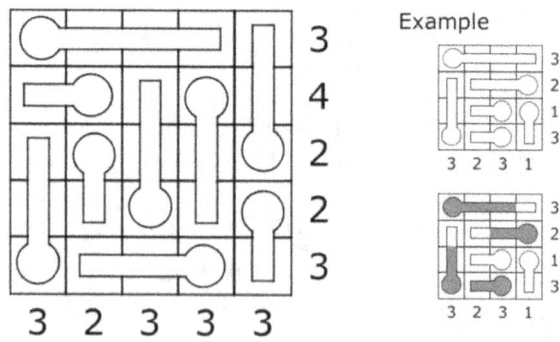

16   Mathemagic Puzzles & Brain Drainers

Puzzle 27

Tommy: "How old are you, Mamma?"

Mamma: "Let me think, Tommy. Well, our three ages add up to exactly seventy years."

Tommy: "That's a lot, isn't it? And how old are you, Papa?"

Papa: "Just six times as old as you, my son."

Tommy: "Shall I ever be half as old as you, Papa?"

Papa: "Yes, Tommy; and when that happens our three ages will add up to exactly twice as much as today."

Tommy: "And supposing I was born before you, Papa; and supposing Mamma had forgot all about it, and hadn't been at home when I came; and supposing..."

Mamma: "Supposing, Tommy, we talk about bed. Come along, darling. You'll have a headache."

Now, if Tommy had been some years older, he might have calculated the exact ages of his parents from the information they had given him. Can you find out the exact age of Mamma?

Puzzle 28

Fred can eat 27 chocolates in an hour, Alice can eat 2 chocolates in 10 minutes, and Kelly can eat 7 chocolates in 20 minutes. How long will it take them to share and eat a large box of 120 chocolates whilst watching a movie?

In one hour, Fred eats 27 chocolates, Alice eats 12, and Kelly eats 21. A total of 60 chocolates. Therefore 120 chocolates would take 120 ÷ 60 = 2 hours.

Puzzle 29
Each empty white square in the grid contains one of the numbers 1, 2, 3,..., 8. Each of the horizontal and vertical equations must be true and each number must be used exactly once.

	÷		=	
+		×		
	+		=	
=		=		

Puzzle 30
Which country is hidden in the paragraph below?

Aliens landed in downtown Chicago last night. Most locals stepped outside to see the spaceship's massive wingspan. Amazingly, seven people failed to see the sight before them, as they took shelter from the great light that shone from upon high.

Puzzle 31
What is half of two plus two?

Puzzle 32

Add lines to this grid and create five areas that each have 4 letters, to spell five 4-lettered words.

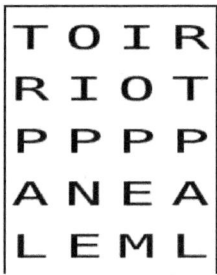

Puzzle 33

Can you draw a line through all of the edges in this picture?

Each side is broken into 2 or 3 edges, and there are also 7 edges inside that you have to cross. The line must be continuous, and cross each edge exactly once.

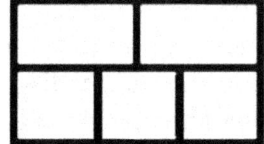

Puzzle 34

Moving up or right, what is the highest total you can make, using the mathematical signs along the way?

+	4	–	2	+	2
2	+	2	–	2	+
–	1	+	2	–	4
2	–	1	+	1	–
+	1	–	2	+	3
3	+	3	–	4	+

Puzzle 35

Which of the five black shapes is identical to the red one? There may be more than one which is exactly the same.

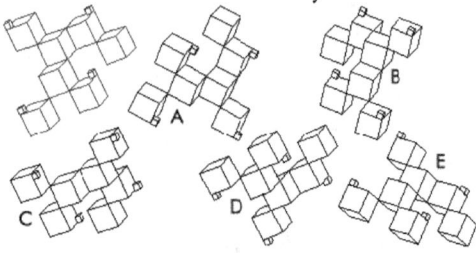

Puzzle 36

Can you find a seven-digit-number which describes itself. The first digit is the number of zeros in the number. The second digit is the number of ones in the number, etc. For example, in the number 21200, there are 2 zeros, 1 one, 2 twos, 0 threes and 0 fours.

Puzzle 37

Your objective is to place some diagonal 'mirrors' into the grid.

If a ray of light is shone in to the grid from each of the letters, and allowed to bounce off the internal diagonal mirrors, each will exit the grid at the twin of the letter that it entered the grid. For example, a ray entering at either letter D will bounce off some mirrors and exit the grid at the other letter D.

Each row and each column will contain exactly two of the diagonal mirrors.

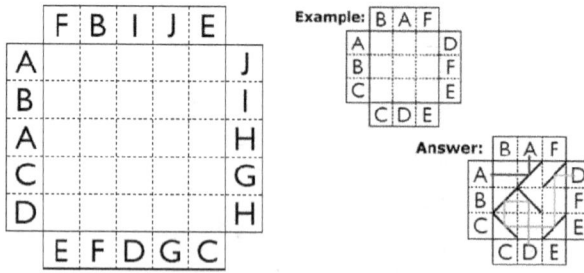

Puzzle 38
How can you get ten horses into nine stables, one per stable?

Puzzle 39
Last week, I travelled from London to Stoke. On the first day, I travelled one half of the distance. On day two, I travelled one third of the remaining distance. On day three, I travelled three quarters of the remaining distance. Yesterday, I travelled one half of the remaining distance. I now have 5 miles left to travel. How far is it from Stoke to London in total?

Puzzle 40
Fill in the missing numbers with the digits 1 to 9. A diamond shape in the middle means that the four numbers around it add to 20.

Each uses a different way to add to 20, i.e., if there is already 1 + 3 + 8 + 9, then there will not be another using the digits 1, 3, 8 and 9 (in any order). The same digit isn't allowed to touch, even diagonally.

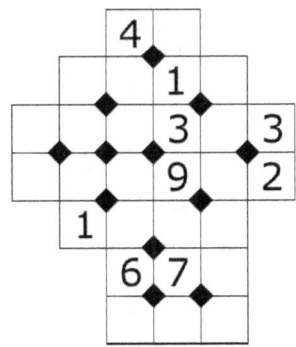

Puzzle 41

The Miller next took the company aside and showed them nine sacks of fl our that were standing as depicted in the sketch. "Now, hearken, all and some," said he, "while that I do set ye the riddle of the nine sacks of fl our. And mark ye, my lords and masters, that there be single sacks on the outside, pairs next unto them, and three together in the middle thereof. By Saint Benedict, it doth so happen that if we do but multiply the pair, 28, by the single one, 7, the answer is 196, which is of a truth the number shown by the sacks in the middle. Yet it be not true that the other pair, 34, when so multiplied by its neighbour, 5, will also make 196. Wherefore I do beg you, gentle sirs, so to place anew the nine sacks with as little trouble as possible that each pair when thus multiplied by its single neighbour shall make the number in the middle." As the Miller has stipulated in effect that as few bags as possible shall be moved, there is only one answer to this puzzle, which everybody should be able to solve.

TEST YOUR BRAIN POWER!

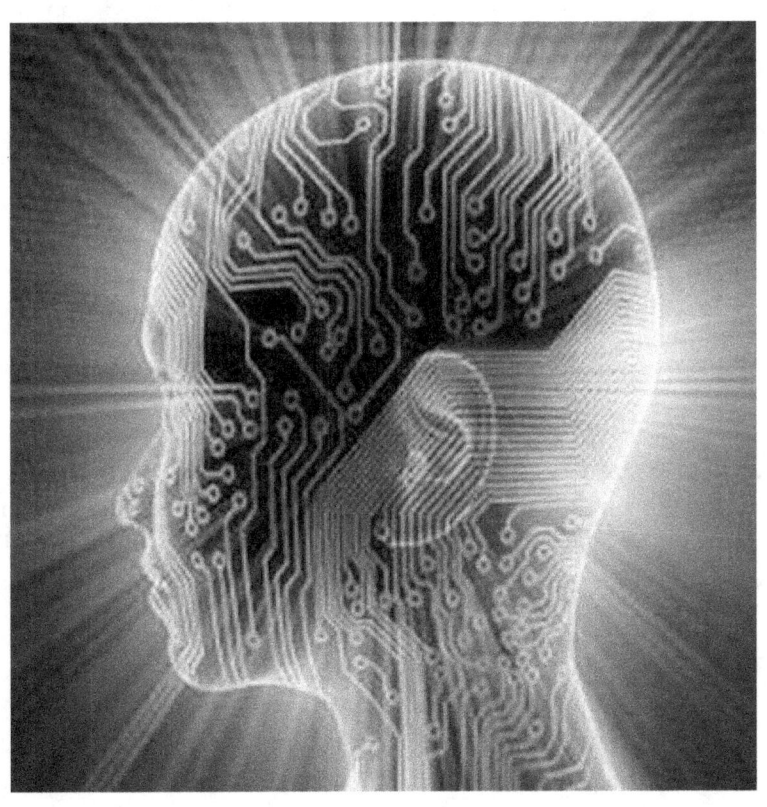

Brainteasers

Ready to give your brain a little exercise? See if you can solve the brainteasers. Good luck!

Brainteaser 1
You're standing at three light switches at the bottom of the stairs to the attic. Each one corresponds to one of the three lights in the attic, but you cannot see the lights from where you stand. You can turn the switches on and off and leave them in any position. How can you identify which switch corresponds to which light bulb if you are only allowed one trip upstairs?

Brainteaser 2
A man is trapped in a room with only two possible exits: two doors. Through the first door, there is a room constructed from magnifying glass. The blazing sun instantly fries anyone or anything that enters. Through the second door, there is a fire breathing dragon. How does the man escape?

Brainteaser 3
You have a 3 gallon jug and a 5 gallon jug. You need to measure out exactly 7 gallons of water. How do you do it?

Brainteaser 4

You and a good friend go out and have a nice dinner together, and the bill is $25. You and your friend each pay $15 in cash which your Waiter gives to the Cashier. The Cashier hands back $5 to the Waiter. The Waiter keeps $3 as a tip and hands back $1 to each of you. So, you and your friend paid $14 each for the meal, for a total of $28. The Waiter has $3, and that makes $31. Where did the extra dollar come from?

Brainteaser 5

In this puzzle, three numbers: 16, 14 and 38, need to be assigned to one of the rows of numbers below. To which row should each number be assigned?

(Hint: This is not a mathematical problem. The numerical values are irrelevant.)

A	0	6	8	9	3
B	15	27	21	10	19
C	7	1	47	11	17

MIND, MATHS AND LOGIC QUIZZES

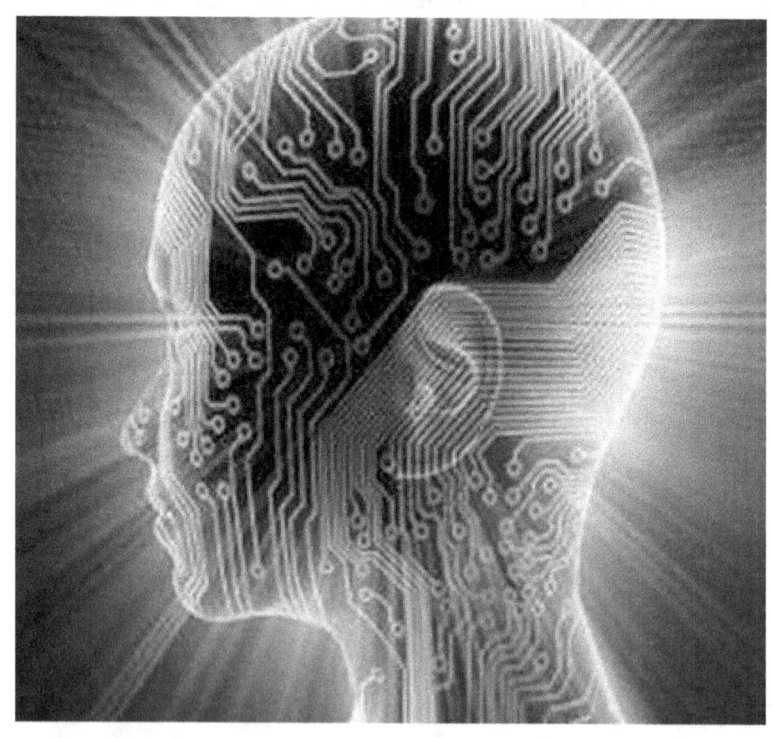

Mind, Maths and Logic Quizzes

Q-1. By moving one of the following digits, make the equation correct. 62 - 63 = 1

Q-2. You have a fox, a chicken and a sack of grain. You must cross a river with only one of them at a time. If you leave the fox with the chicken, he will eat it; if you leave the chicken with the grain, he will eat it. How can you get all the three across safely?

Q-3. You have 12 black socks and 12 white socks mixed up in a drawer. You're up very early and it's too dark to tell them apart. What's the smallest number of socks you need to take out (blindly) to be sure of having a matching pair?

Q-4. What is special about the following sequence of numbers?

8 5 4 9 1 7 6 10 3 2 0

Q-5. Three travellers register at a hotel and are told that their rooms will cost $10 each, so they pay $30. Later the clerk realises that he made a mistake and should have only charged them $25. He gives a bellboy $5 to return to them, but the bellboy is dishonest and gives them each only $1, keeping $2 for himself. So the men actually spent $27 and the bellboy kept $2. What happened to the other dollar of the original $30?

Q-6. You are the bus driver. At your first stop, you pick up 29 people. On your second stop, 18 of those 29 people get off, and

at the same time, 10 new passengers arrive. At your next stop, 3 of those 10 passengers get off, and 13 new passengers come on. On your fourth stop, 4 of the remaining 10 passengers get off, 6 of those new 13 passengers get off as well, then 17 new passengers get on. What is the colour of the bus driver's eyes?

Q-7. A rooster lays an egg at the very top of a slanted roof. Which side is the egg going to roll off on?

Q-8. U2 has a concert that starts in 17 minutes and they must all cross a bridge to get there. All four men begin on the same side of the bridge. You must help them across to the other side. It is night. There is one fl ashlight. A maximum of two people can cross at one time. Any party who crosses, either 1 or 2 people, must have the fl ashlight with them.
The fl ashlight must be walked back and forth. It cannot be thrown and other tricks like that are not needed to solve the problem. The solution is simply a matter of allocating resources in a certain order. Each band member walks at a different speed. A pair must walk together at the rate of the slower man's pace:
Bono: 1 minute to cross
Edge: 2 minutes to cross
Adam: 5 minutes to cross
Larry: 10 minutes to cross
For example: If Bono and Larry walk across fi rst, 10 minutes have elapsed when they get to the other side of the bridge. If Larry then returns with the fl ashlight, a total of 20 minutes have passed and you have failed the mission.

Q-9. Why is it very common to have a 9-minute snooze interval on alarm clocks, why not 10 instead?

Q-10. A bookworm eats from the fi rst page of an encyclopedia to the last page in a straight line. The encyclopedia consists of ten 1000-page volumes and is sitting on a bookshelf in the usual

order. Not counting covers, title pages, etc., how many pages does the bookworm eat through?

```
B | |              |  |F
A |1|..............|10|R
C | |              |  |O
K | |              |  |N
  |_|              |__|T
```

Q-11. An Arab sheikh tells his two sons to race their camels to a distant city to see who will inherit his fortune. The one whose camel is slower will win. The brothers, after wandering aimlessly for days, ask a wise man for advice. After hearing the advice, they jump on the camels and race as fast as they can to the city. What does the wise man say?

Q-12. An 18-wheeler is crossing a 4-kilometre bridge that can only support 10,000 kilograms and that's exactly how much the rig weighs. Halfway across the bridge a 30-gram sparrow lands on the cab, but the bridge doesn't collapse. Why not?

Q-13. A completely black dog was strolling down Main Street during a total blackout affecting the entire town. Not a single streetlight had been on for hours. Just as the dog was crossing the middle line, a Buick Skylark with two broken headlights speedily approaches his position, but manages to swerve out of the way just in time. How could the driver have possibly seen the dog to swerve in time?

Q-14. In a small cabin in the woods, two men lay dead. The cabin itself is not burnt, but the forest all around is burnt to cinders. How did the men die?

Q-15. Ida puts her coffee into the microwave, as she does every morning, for exactly 2 minutes. When the microwave goes off, she opens the door, but then closes the door again and sets

the microwave for 2 more seconds. What good would 2 more seconds be?

Q-16. Beulah died in the Appalachians while Craig died at sea. Everyone was much happier with Craig's death. Why?

Q-17. You are a cook in a remote area with no clocks or other way of keeping time other than a four-minute and a seven-minute hourglass. On the stove is a pot of boiling water. Jill asks you for a nine-minute egg, and you know she is a perfectionist and can tell if you undercook or overcook the egg by even a few seconds. How can you cook the egg for exactly 9 minutes?

Q-18. I am the owner of a pet store. If I put in one canary per cage, I have one bird too many. If I put in two canaries per cage, I have one cage too many. How many cages and canaries do I have?

Q-19. Here is a series of numbers. What is the next number in the sequence?

$$1$$
$$11$$
$$21$$
$$1211$$
$$111221$$
$$312211$$
$$13112221$$

Q-20. My daughter has many sisters. She has as many sisters as she has brothers. Each of her brothers has twice as many sisters as brothers. How many sons and daughters do I have?

Q-21. Tom's mother has three children. One is named April, one is named May. What is the third one named?

Q-22. Two women apply for a job. They are identical and have the same mother, father and birthday. The interviewer asks, "Are you twins?" to which they honestly reply, "No".

How is this possible?

Q-23. A boat has a ladder that has six rungs. Each rung is one foot apart. The bottom rung is one foot from the water. The tide rises at 12 inches every 15 minutes. The high tide peaks in one hour.
When the tide is at its highest, how many rungs are under water?

Q-24. You have a lighter and two fuses that take exactly one hour to burn, but they don't burn at a steady rate. For example, one fuse could take 59 minutes to burn the first inch and then burn the rest of the fuse in the last minute.
How would you use these two fuses to measure 45 minutes?

Q-25. You have two buckets – one holds exactly 5 gallons and the other 3 gallons. How can you measure 4 gallons of water into the 5-gallon bucket?
(Assume you have an unlimited supply of water and that there are no measurement markings of any kind on the buckets.)

Q-26. A princess is as old as the prince will be when the princess is twice the age that the prince was when the princess's age was half the sum of their present ages.
What are their ages?

Q-27. During the World War II, there was a bridge connecting Germany and Switzerland, and on the German side, there was a sentry tower with a guard in it. He would come out every three minutes to check on the bridge, and he had orders to turn back anyone who tried to get into Germany, and shoot anyone trying to escape without a pass. There was a woman, who desperately needed to get into Switzerland, and she knew she didn't have time to get a pass. It would take her at least six minutes to cross the bridge, but she managed to do it. How?

Q-28. A man can make perfect counterfeit bills. They look exactly like real ones, they're made of exactly the same materials, made the same way, everything. So perfect, one could pretty

much call them real bills. One day he successfully makes a perfect copy of another bill. However, he gets caught when he tries to use the copy. How is this possible?

Q-29. A prisoner is told, "If you tell a lie, we will hang you; if you tell the truth, we will shoot you." What can he say to save himself?

Q-30. How many people can read hex if only you and dead people can read hex?

Q-31. A man is looking at a picture of a man on the wall and states: Brothers and sisters I have none, but this man's father is my father's son. Who is the man in the picture in relation to the man looking at the picture?

Q-32. A man and his son had a terrible car accident and were rushed to the hospital. The man died on the way, but the son was still barely alive. When they arrived, an old, grey surgeon was called in to operate. Upon seeing the young boy, the surgeon said, "I can't operate – this is my son."
How is this possible?

Q-33. A wise king devised a contest to see who would receive the Princess' hand in marriage. The Princess was put in a 50 × 50 foot carpeted room. Each of her four suitors were put in one corner of the room with a small box to stand on. The first one to touch the Princess' hand would be the winner and become the new King.

The rules were the contestants could not walk over the carpet, cross the plane of the carpet, or hang from anything; nor could they use anything but their bodies and wits (i.e., no magic, telepathy, nor any items, such as ladders, blocks and tackles, etc.). One suitor figured out a way and married the Princess and became the new King. What did he do?

Q-34. Two guards were on duty outside a barrack. One faced up the road to watch for anyone approaching from the North.

The other looked down the road to see if anyone approached from the South. Suddenly one of them said to the other, "Why are you smiling?"
How did he know his companion was smiling?

Q-35. You're riding a horse. To the right of you is a cliff and in front of you is an elephant moving at the same pace and you can't overtake it. To the left of you is a hippo running at the same speed and a lion is chasing you. How do you get to safety?

Q-36. You have 50 quarters on the table in front of you. You are blindfolded and cannot discern whether a coin is heads up or tails up by feeling it. You are told that x coins are heads up, where $0 < x < 50$. You are asked to separate the coins into two piles in such a way that the number of heads up coins in both piles is the same at the end. You may fl ip any coin over as many times as you want. How will you do it?

Q-37. You have four chains. Each chain has three links in it. Although it is diffi cult to cut the links, you wish to make a single loop with all the 12 links. What is the fewest number of cuts you must make to accomplish this task?

Q-38. Three closed boxes have either white marbles, black marbles or both, and they are labelled white, black and both. However, you're told that each of the labels are wrong. You may reach into one of the boxes and pull out only one marble. Which box should you remove a marble from to determine the contents of all the three boxes?

Q-39. A glass of water with a single ice cube sits on a table. When the ice has completely melted, will the level of the water have increased, decreased or remain unchanged?

Q-40. You are given eight coins and told that one of them is counterfeit. The counterfeit one is slightly heavier than the

other seven. Otherwise, the coins look identical. Using a simple balance scale, how can you determine which coin is counterfeit using the scale only twice?

Q-41. I was visiting a friend one evening and remembered that he had three daughters. I asked him how old they were. "The product of their ages is 72," he answered. Quizzically, I asked, "Is there anything else you can tell me?" "Yes," he replied, "the sum of their ages is equal to the number of my house." I stepped outside to see what the house number was. Upon returning inside, I said to my host, "I'm sorry, but I still can't fi gure out their ages." He responded apologetically, "I'm sorry, I forgot to mention that my oldest daughter likes strawberry shortcake." With this information, I was able to determine all three of their ages. How old is each daughter?

Q-42. You're in a room with two doors. There's a guard at each door. One door is the exit, but behind the other door is something that will kill you. You're told that one guard always tells the truth and the other guard always lies. You don't know which guard is which. You are allowed to ask one question to either of the guards to determine which door is the exit. What question should you ask?

Q-43. How far can a dog run into the forest?

Q-44. What number comes next?
$$2, 2, 4, 12, 48, \_\_\_$$

Q-45. You are a prisoner sentenced to death. The Emperor offers you a chance to live by playing a simple game. He gives you 50 black marbles, 50 white marbles and 2 empty bowls and instructs you to divide the 100 marbles into the two bowls. You can divide them however you want as long as all the marbles are in the bowls. You will be blindfolded and the bowls and marbles will be throughly mixed. You will then choose a single marble

from one of the bowls. If the marble is white, you live. Black and you will be put to death.
How do you divide the marbles up so that you have the greatest probability of choosing a white marble?

Q-46. What is the next number in this series?
$$1, 2, 6, 42, 1806?$$

Q-47. If:
$$2\ 3 = 10$$
$$7\ 2 = 63$$
$$6\ 5 = 66$$
$$8\ 4 = 96$$
$$9\ 7 = ??$$

Q-48. What do the following numerals represent?
$$11111121113122223222$$

Q-49. You must buy 100 chickens for exactly $100, and purchase at least one chicken from each store. The first store charges 5 cents/chicken, the second charges $1/chicken and the third charges $5/chicken. How many chickens should you buy from each store?

Q-50. What is special about the following number sequence?
$$8, 5, 4, 9, 1, 7, 6, 10, 3, 2, 0$$

Q-51. Which two numbers are missing and where do they go in the sequence?
$$8, 11, 5, 14, 1, 7, 6, 10, 13, 3, 12, 2$$

Q-52. What 4-digit number abcd satisfies this equation?
$$4 * abcd = dcba$$

Q-53. Bill buys three items at the store for exactly $100. The second item costs half as much as the first item, and the third item is half as much as the second. How much did each one cost?

Q-54. A man was killed on Sunday morning. His wife found the body and called the police. The police arrived and questioned the chef, maid, butler and the gardener. Their alibis were:

Chef - making breakfast
Maid - getting mail
Butler - setting table
Gardener - watering plants

The police immediately arrested the criminal. Who was it and how did they know?

Q-55. This is an unusual paragraph. I'm curious as to just how quickly you can find out what is so unusual about it. It looks so ordinary and plain that you would think nothing was wrong with it. In fact, nothing is wrong with it! It is highly unusual though. Study it and think about it, but you still may not find anything odd. But if you work at it a bit, you might find out. Try to do so without any coaching.

Q-56. A murderer is condemned to death. He has to choose between the three rooms. The first is full of raging fires, the second is full of assassins with loaded guns, and the third is full of lions that haven't eaten for 3 years. Which room is safest for him?

Q-57. Name three consecutive days without using the words, Wednesday, Friday, or Sunday.

Q-58. There are six glasses in a row. The first three are full of water, and the next three are empty. By moving only one glass, how can you make them alternate between full and empty?

Q-59. What four weights can be used to balance from 1 to 30 pounds?

Q-60. Given these equations, what is the answer to the last one?
5 3 2 = 151012
9 2 4 = 183662
8 6 3 = 482466
5 4 5 = 202504
7 2 5 = ?

Q-61. 44 33 555 555 666 9 666 777 555 3
What is the message in this code?

Q-62. Two men are standing on one side of a bridge and two women are approaching them. One of the men says, "Here comes my wife and daughter," to which the second man replies, "Here comes my wife and daughter." If they have not married the same woman and the women aren't pregnant, how is this true?

Q-63. Rearrange the letters in the words, "new door" to make one word.

Q-64. Two fathers and two sons go fishing together in the same boat. They all catch a fish but the total catch for the day is 3 fishes. How is this possible?

Q-65. A green glass door admits only certain objects. Apples and balls are allowed, but pears and bats aren't. What determines whether an item can enter?

Q-66. B,C,D,E,G,P
What is the next letter in the sequence?

Q-67. A mile-long train is moving at sixty miles an hour when it reaches a mile-long tunnel. How long does it take the entire train to pass through the tunnel?

Q-68. First, think of the colour of the clouds. Next think of the colour of the snow. Last, think of the colour of the moon. Now, what do cows drink?

Q-69. Rhonda will go see ballet but not the opera. Her favourite number is eight and she doesn't like nine. She likes salmon but not trout. She hates Mondays and likes Wednesdays. Does she use a comb or a brush?

Q-70. On a regular 12-hour digital clock, how many times would the same three digits in a row be displayed (e.g. 1:11, 11:12, 12:22) in one day?

Q-71. A man says his dog can jump over his house. No one believes him but he is right. How is that possible?

Q-72. Five pigeons are sitting on a fence. The farmer comes out and shoots one. How many are left?

Q-73. A plane with 50 passengers crashes and everyone is killed, but there were only 49 bodies. How is this possible?

Q-74. A man leaves home, turns left, goes straight, turns left again, goes straight and turns left once more, then returns home and there's another man with a mask on. What's going on?

Q-75. A man is leaving on a business trip and stops by his office on the way to the airport. The night watchman stops him and says, "Sir, don't take that flight. I had a dream last night that your plane would crash and everyone would die!" The businessman cancels his trip and sure enough, the plane crashes, killing all the passengers. The man gives his watchman a $10,000 reward for saving his life, then fires him. Why?

Q-76. If you were to spell out the numbers, how far would you have to go before encountering the letter 'A'?

Q-77. A sharpshooter hangs up his hat, turns around and walks 50 metres, then turns around and shoots his gun, putting a hole right through his hat. How did he do it?

Q-78. 5 cats can catch 5 mice in 5 minutes. How many cats does it take to catch 100 mice in 100 minutes?

Q-79. You are in a room with no windows, doors or any exit. The only items are a mirror and a table. How do you escape? (Not a typical brainteaser)

Q-80. There's a green ranch house on a green street with green walls, tables and chairs. What colour is the staircase?

Q-81. A man saw a snake crossing the road and swerved to crush it with his tires. All the street-lights were off as well as the car's headlights. There were no other lights on along the road. How did the man see the snake?

Q-82. What do the following words have in common?
current, by, dew, faze, loan, ate

Q-83. How can you alter the following equation by a single stroke to make it correct?
5 + 5 + 5 = 550

Q-84. During lunch hour, a group of boys from Mr. Bryant's homeroom visited a nearby grocery store. One of the five took an apple.
Jim said, "It was Hank or Tom."
Hank said, "Neither Eddie nor I did it."
Tom said, "Both of you are lying."
Don said, "No, one of them is lying, the other is speaking the truth."
Eddie said, "No, Don, that is not true."
When Mr. Bryant was consulted, he said, "Three of these boys are always truthful but two will lie every time."
Who took the apple?

Q-85. A six-digit number represented by ABCDEF (each letter represents a different number) can be multiplied by 2, 3, 4, 5, and 6 and yet no new digits appear in the result. As a matter of fact, all the digits are rotated. What is the number?

Q-86. What do these represent?
24 = HiaD
26 = LotA
7 = DotW
9 = LoaC
12 = SotZ
88 = PK

Q-87. How do you pronounce Ghoti?

Q-88. What does this sentence represent?

    Stand   Take   Mine   Taking
      I   You   To   My

Q-89. What is the only anagram of Springiest?

Q-90. How do you turn 2 into 5?

Q-91. What is N?

                6, 9, 27, 54, N, 2241

Q-92. Two boys weighing 50 pounds each and their older brother weighing 100 pounds wish to cross a river. Their boat will only hold 100 pounds. How can they all cross the river in the boat?

Q-93. A circular island with a diameter of 30 feet has a 30 feet tree standing at the centre. A man cuts the tree down with his chain-saw, making the cut a foot up from the ground. The tree comes crashing down and hits the water but doesn't splash. Why not?

Q-94. Jack is looking at Anne, but Anne is looking at George. Jack is married, but George is not. Is a married person looking at an unmarried person?
A) Yes
B) No
C) Cannot be determined

Q-95. What is the missing number?
                2 3 4 15 12
                3 4 5 28 20
                4 5 6 45 30
                5 6 7 66 42
                6 7 8 ?? 56

Q-96. Two scruffy dogs were walking down the street. The first dog turned to the other and said, "Do you realise that if one of your fleas jumped onto me, we would have the same number of fleas?" The second replied, "Yes, but if one of your fleas jumped onto me I would have five times as many fleas as you." How many fleas are on each dog to begin with?

Q-97. A snail creeps 10 feet up a wall during the daytime, then falls asleep. It wakes up the next morning and discovers it slipped down 6 feet. If this happens each day, how many days will it take to reach the top of a 22-feet wall?

Q-98. Two children were playing checkers and each played five games. Both children won the same number of games, yet there were no ties. How is this possible?

Q-99. How can you put 21 pigs in 4 pigpens and still have an odd number of pigs in each pen?

Q-100. A woman gave a man a list of things she needed to buy at the store. The man gave the list back to the woman and she turned red with embarrassment. Why?

Q-101. Mike, Jimmy, Nader, Kevin and Larry were the top five finishers in the regional 500-mile race. They drove yellow, orange, green, red and blue cars, but not necessarily in that order. Neither Kevin nor Larry drove the green car. Kevin finished faster than Mike and Larry. The blue car finished earlier than Larry's and Nader's car. The yellow car finished faster than the green car and the orange car. Mike's and Larry's car finished ahead of the orange car. Jimmy's car finished before the blue and the yellow car. Who drove what colour car and what place did each driver finish?

Q-102. While driving his car, a man slams on the brakes when he sees, in the middle of the street, a diamond studded door, a gold door and a silver door. Which door does he open first?

Q-103. Ronald has a rare opportunity to meet the President of the United States. During his visit, the President gives him a gift but tells Ronald, he is never to sell it unless he sees the President again. Ronald consents, but the President dies later that year. Years later, a man offers to buy the President's gift for $1000. Ronald agrees and exchanges the gift for 20 crisp $50 bills. Did he keep his promise?

Q-104. What 3-digit number has a tens digit that is 5 more than the ones digit and a hundreds digit that is 8 less than the tens digit?

Q-105. Why are manhole covers round?

Q-106. You are in the woods with owls and wolves. There are 22 eyes and 32 legs. How many owls and wolves are there?

Q-107. When can ten plus ten equal ten, yet ten minus ten equal twenty?

Q-108. Eat fl ush to my nose tree times for they buy dead by too. What is the answer?

Q-109. A man owed his friend $63 and repaid him the exact amount in cash without using coins or $1 bills (no online transfers, cheques, credit cards or any other tricks) and without requiring change. How did he do it?

Q-110. Perform this calculation in your head, mentally adding the numbers as quickly as you can. Start with 1000 and add 40. Now add 1000. Add 30 to that, then add another 1000. Now add 20 to that result. Add another 1000 and fi nally, add 10 to that. What is the total?

Q-111. Read this sentence.
   Finished files are the result of years of scientif-
   ic study combined with
   the experience of years.
How many times does the letter 'F' appear?

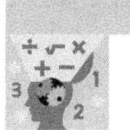

Q-112. Without changing the order of these numbers, how can they equal to 100?

3 5 6 2 54 5

Q-113. A taxi driver runs through four red lights, two stop signs and goes through a house. A police officer witnesses this but doesn't do anything. Why not?

Q-114. Suppose you have twelve eggs and a balance scale. All of the eggs are identical except for one, whose only difference is its weight. Using the scale only three times, determine which egg is the odd egg out and whether it is heavier or lighter than the other eggs.

Q-115. What number belongs at the beginning of this sequence?
?, 3, 2, 3, 9, 2, 4, 8, 4, 3, 7, 6

Q-116. A clock loses exactly ten minutes every hour. If the clock is set correctly at noon, what is the correct time when the clock reads 3:00pm?

Q-117. A man is running across a field at night clutching something in his arms as several other men pursue him. He looks back and sees they're getting closer. In a final burst of effort, his pursuers catch up and bring him crashing to the ground. His pursuers stand over him but do not touch him or take what he was carrying. Why not? Who was the running man?

Q-118. Two cowboys live next door to each other and both have a corral for their cows in the back. One day, they meet at the back of their homes, standing next to a wall dividing their corrals. The first cowboy gets to thinking and asks his neighbour for a cow so that he can double his herd. The other cowboys reply, "That's fine by me partner, cuz then we'll have the same number of cows?" How many cows does each cowboy own?

Q-119. On a dark, stormy, Halloween night, four kids named Luke, John, Sarah and Bob walk into a haunted house during

a blackout. Only one can escape. They take a staircase to the second floor, a trapdoor on the left, then go up the ladder to the right, followed by a 28-feet slide to the basement through the mouth of a Giant Panda. In one corner of the murky cellar is a chain-saw, a dagger, a rope with a noose and an electric chair. Written on the wall in blood are the words, "Only one will survive - choose your death!" Bob takes the rope, Sarah picks up the dagger, John chooses the chain-saw and Luke uses the chair.

Who survives?

Q-120. What does this represent?

        Pot OOOOOOOO

Q-121. Given the numbers – 1, 6, 7 and 9, find an equation that equals to 24. You may only use each digit once.

Q-122. A red-house is made of red bricks, has a red wooden door and a red roof. A yellow-house is made of yellow bricks, has a yellow wooden door and a yellow roof. What is a green-house made of?

Q-123. On a game show, there are three closed doors - one hides a car and the other two conceal a goat. The contestant selects a door, which remains closed, and the host, knowing where the car is hidden, reveals a goat behind one of the remaining two doors. The contestant is then given the option to switch doors or stay with the one they originally selected. What should the contestant do to have the best chance of winning the car?

Q-124. If a plane sits on a conveyer belt whose speed matches that of the plane in the opposite direction, can the plane take off?

Q-125. Three rooms contain, 1) Gold coins, 2) Currency notes and 3) Cotton bags. If all the three rooms catch fire, which room will the ambulance pour water on first?

Q-126. Alfred and Bill are clerks at the local grocery store. Alfred can stock a shelf in 20 minutes, but Bill is new and takes 30 minutes. How long would it take for them to stock a shelf together?

Q-127. Ralph goes to the hardware store to buy something for his house. He asks the clerk how much will one cost and the clerk looks it up and tells him – it will be $3. He asks about buying twelve and is told, it will be $6. Two hundred will cost $9. What is Ralph buying?

BRAIN DRAINERS

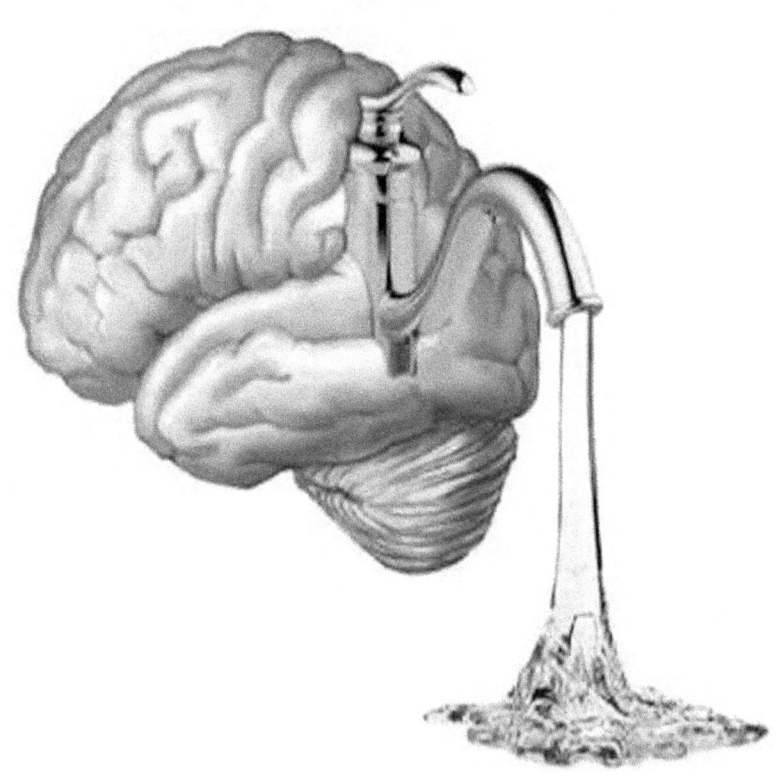

Brain Drainers

Q-1. You are a cyclist in a cross-country race. Just before the crossing finish line, you overtake the person in second place! What place did you finish in?

Q-2. In a year, there are 12 months. 7 months have 31 days. How many months have 28 days?

Q-3. A plane crashes on the border of the U.S. and Canada. Where do they bury the survivors?

Q-4. I do not have any special powers, but I can predict the score of any football game before it begins. How can I do this?

Q-5. You are on the bank of a river. You have to get a fox, a hen, and corn to the other side of the river. If left alone, the fox will eat the hen, the hen will also eat the corn, if left alone. The boat is only big enough to take you and one of the other three to the other side. How do you get all the three across intact?

Q-6. Please add the following numbers mentally.

Start with 1000.
Add 40
Add 1000
Add 30
Add 1000
Add 20

Add 1000
Add 10

Write down your answer.

Q-7. In baseball, how many outs are there in an inning?

Q-8. I have 2 U.S. coins that total 55 cents. One of them is not a nickel. What are the 2 coins?

Q-9. Jimmy's mother had 4 children. She named the first Monday. Named the second Tuesday. The third is named Wednesday. What is the name of the fourth child?

Q-10. You are driving a bus. At the first stop, 2 women get on. The second stop, 3 men get on and 1 woman gets off. Third stop, 3 kids and their mom get on, and a man gets off. The bus is grey, and it is raining outside. What colour is the bus driver's hair?

Q-11. Before Mt. Everest was discovered, which was the highest mountain in the world?

Q-12. I left my campsite and hiked south for 3 miles. Turned east and hiked for 3 miles. Then turned north and hiked for 3 miles, at which time, I came upon a bear inside my tent eating my food!
What colour was the bear?

Q-13. A man lives on the fifteenth floor of an apartment building. Every morning, he takes the elevator down to the lobby and leaves the building. In the evening, he gets into the elevator, and, if there is someone else in the elevator, or if it was raining that day, he goes back to his floor directly. Otherwise, he goes to the tenth floor and walks up five flights of stairs to his apartment. Can you explain why he does this?

Q-14. Crime Scene: A large wooden box was built with one door. The door was locked from inside, and then nailed shut from the inside. The police break into the room. In the middle

of the room, there is a dead man hanging from the ceiling, his feet are 3 feet off the ground. The only other thing in the room is a hammer lying in a puddle of water. Can you explain what happened?

Q-15. Alex wants to go home but can't, because the man in the mask is waiting for him. What is going on?

Q-16. Your sock drawer contains 24 white socks and 30 black socks. The lights in your room are off, so you cannot see the colour of the socks. How many socks must you grab to ensure to have at least one matching pair?

Q-17. You are in a cookie factory, and need to make a huge batch of chocolate chip cookies. The recipe calls for exactly 4 cups of sugar. Problem is that you have two buckets. One is 5 cups, the other is 3 cups. Using these buckets, can you measure exactly 4 cups of sugar? How?

Q-18. A man is the owner of a winery who recently passed away. In his will, he left 21 barrels (seven of which are filled with wine, seven of which are half full, and seven of which are empty) to his three sons. However, the wine and barrels must be split so that each son has the same number of full barrels, the same number of half-full barrels, and the same number of empty barrels. Note that there are no measuring devices handy. How can the barrels and wine be evenly divided?

Q-19. An Arab Sheikh is old and must will his fortune to one of his two sons. He makes a proposition. His two sons will ride their camels in a race, and whichever camel crosses the finish line LAST will win the fortune for its owner. During the race, the two brothers wander aimlessly for days, neither willing to cross the finish line. In desperation, they ask a wise man for advice. He tells them something; then the brothers leap onto the camels and charge towards the finish line. What did the wise man say?

Q-20. You have a 3-gallon jug and a 5-gallon jug. You need to measure out exactly 7-gallons of water. How can you do it?

Q-21. A man is on a game show. He is presented with two doors, one on the left, and one on the right. Behind one is 2 million dollars, and behind the other is a donkey. Choose the correct door to win the prize. There are also two men in front of the doors, and they know which door leads to the millions. One wears a black hat, the other wears a white hat.
The host explains that one of the men is a liar, and will always lie, and the other man will always tell the truth - but you don't know which is which.
You can ask only one of the men only one question. What is the question, and which man do you ask to ensure you win the money?

Q-22. You and two friends rent a hotel room that costs $30, so you put in $10 each. Later that night, the owner of the hotel realises he has overcharged you, so he sends the bellhop with $5. The bellhop steals $2 and returns $1 to each of you.
So you each have now paid $9. $9 × 3 = $27. The bellhop stole $2. That equals $29 – what happened to the last dollar?

Q-23. Three men are captured by cannibals in the jungle. The men are given one chance to escape with their lives. The men are lined up and bound to stakes, such that one man can see the backs of the other two, the middle man can see the back of the front man, and the front man can't see anybody. The men are shown five hats, three of which are black and two of which are white. Then the men are blindfolded, and one of the five hats is placed on each man's head. The remaining two hats are hidden away. The blindfolds are removed. The men are told that if just one of the men can guess which hat he's wearing, they may all go free. Time passes. Finally, the front man, who can't see anyone, correctly guesses the colour of his hat. What colour was it, and how did he guess correctly?

Q-24. A man is looking at a photograph of someone. His friend asks who it is. The man replies, "Brothers and sisters, I have none. But that man's father is my father's son." Who was in the photograph?

Q-25. What can run but never walks, has a mouth but never speaks, has a head but never weeps, and has a bed but never sleeps?

Q-26. A man left home running. He ran a ways and then turned left, ran the same distance and turned left again, ran the same distance and turned left again. When he got home, there were two masked men. Who were they?

Q-27. What is full of holes but can still hold water?

Q-28. Your dad tells you that he will pay you 6.00₹ an hour for the 6 seconds that you take to wash your hands before dinner. How much did you make for washing your hands?

MATH RIDDLES

Math Riddles

A collection of Math Riddles for fun and pleasure! Tease your brain with these riddles.

Riddle-1
Why should you never mention the number 288 in front of anyone?

Riddle-2
Which weighs more? A pound of iron or a pound of feathers?

Riddle-3
How is the moon like a dollar?

Riddle-4
What is alive and has only 1 foot?

Riddle-5
When do giraffes have 8 feet?

Riddle-6
How many eggs can you put in an empty basket?

Riddle-7
What coin doubles in value when half is deducted?

Riddle-8
What is the difference between a new penny and an old quarter?

Riddle-9
If you can buy eight eggs for 26 cents, how many can you buy for a cent and a quarter?

Riddle-10
Where can you buy a ruler that is 3 feet long?

Riddle-11
If there were 9 cats on a bridge and one jumped over the edge, how many would be left?

Riddle-12
If you take three apples from five apples, how many do you have?

Riddle-13
What has 4 legs and only 1 foot?

Riddle-14
How many times can you subtract 6 from 30?

Riddle-15
If one nickel is worth five cents, how much is half of one-half of a nickel worth?

Riddle-16
How many 9's are there between 1 and 100?

Riddle-17
Which is more valuable – one pound of $10 gold coins or half a pound of $20 gold coins?

Riddle-18
It happens once in a minute, twice in a week, and once in a year. What is it?

Riddle-19
How can half of 12 be 7?

Riddle-20
When things go wrong, what can you always count on?

Riddle-21
Why are diapers like 100 dollar bills?

Riddle-22
A street that is 40 yards long has a tree every 10 yards on both sides. How many total trees are there on the entire street?

Riddle-23
What goes up and never comes down?

Riddle-24
What did one math book say to the other math book?

Riddle-25
Why is the longest human nose on record only 11 inches long?

LOGIC GAMES AND RIDDLES

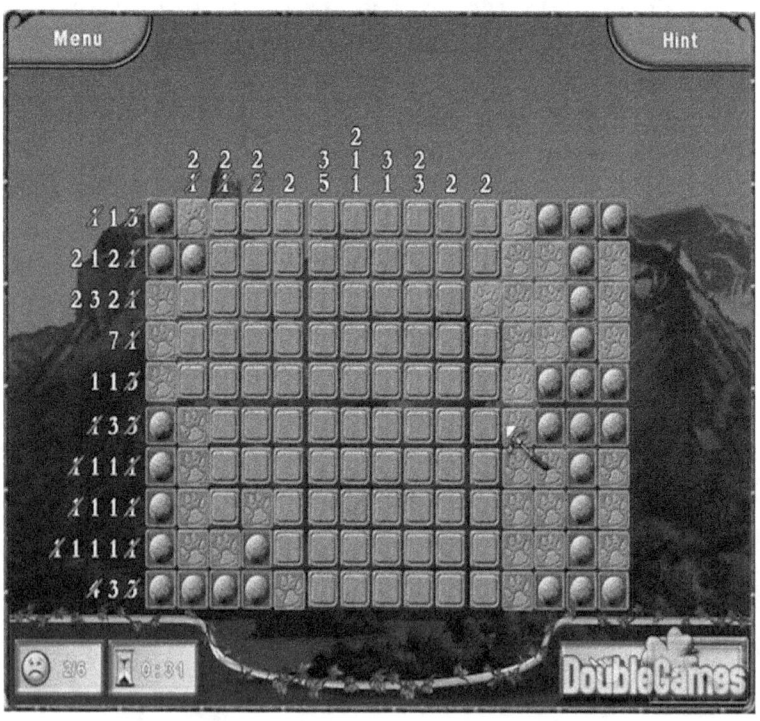

Logic Games and Riddles

1. Riddle
How can you add eight 8's to get the number 1,000? (only use addition)

2. Two Fathers and Two Sons Riddle
Two fathers and two sons sat down to eat eggs for breakfast. They ate exactly three eggs, each person had an egg. The riddle is for you to explain how?

3. Digit Frequency
Part I. What digit is the most frequent between the numbers, 1 and 1,000 (inclusive)?
To solve this riddle, you don't want to manually do all of the math but rather try to fi gure out a pattern.

The most common digit is '1.' Can you fi gure out why? No hints until you try the next riddle because the next riddle is closely tied to this one.

Part II. What digit is the least frequent between the numbers, 1 and 1,000? Answer to Riddle.

4. Three Guys at a Hotel Riddle
Three guys rent a hotel room for the night. When they get to the hotel, they pay the $30 fee, then go up to their room. Soon

the bellhop brings up their bags and gives the lawyers back $5 because the hotel was having a special discount that weekend. So each of the three lawyers decide to keep one of the $5 and to give the bellhop a $2 tip. However, when they sat down to tally up their expenses for the weekend, they could not explain the following details:

Each one of them had originally paid $10 (towards the initial $30), then each got back $1 which meant that they each paid $9. Then they gave the bellhop a $2 tip. HOWEVER, 3 • $9 + $2 = $29

The guys couldn't figure out what happened to the other dollar. After all, the three paid out $30, but could only account for $29.

Can you determine what happened?

5. Foreign Country Riddle
In a certain country, ½ of 5 = 3. If the same proportion holds, what is the value of 1/3 of 10 ?

6. The Merchant
A merchant can place 8 large boxes or 10 small boxes into a carton for shipping. In one shipment, he sent a total of 96 boxes. If there are more large boxes than small boxes, how many cartons did he ship?

7. Crossing the River
A farmer is trying to cross a river. He is taking with him a rabbit, carrots and a fox, and he has a small raft. He can only bring 1 item at a time across the river because his raft can only fit either the rabbit, the carrots or the fox. How does he cross the river? (You can assume that the fox does not eat the rabbit if the man is present, you can also assume that the fox and the rabbit are not trying to escape and run away)

8. Three Brothers on a Farm

Three brothers live in a farm. They agreed to buy new seeds: Adam and Ben would go and Charlie stayed to protect the fi elds. Ben bought 75 sacks of wheat from the market, whereas Adam bought 45 sacks. At home, they split the sacks equally. Charlie had paid 1400 dollars for the wheat. How much dollars did Ben and Adam get of the sum, considering equal split of the sacks?

ANSWERS

Puzzles

Puzzle 1

One weighing is enough.

Take one coin from the first box, two from the second and so on.

When the coins are weighed, the number of 1/16ths light will tell us which box contains the counterfeits.

For example if it was box 5, the weighing would be 5/16 too light.

Puzzle 2

129.

These are the first 10 prime numbers (2, 3, 5...) prefixed with a 1.

Puzzle 3

10.20pm.

Since the clock is gaining 12 minutes every hour, for every real hour that has passed, the clock will show 72 minutes.

Since the clock shows 10.00pm, we know that 22 × 60 = 1320 clock minutes have passed. 1320 ÷ 72 × 60 = 1100.

This therefore equals to 1100 real minutes and hence, 18 hours 20 minutes = 6:20pm.

The clock stopped 4 hours ago, therefore the time must now be 10.20pm.

Puzzle 4
Position officers at B, G and H.

Puzzle 5
4.

The middle of the triangle contains the square root of the sum of the three surrounding numbers.

Puzzle 6
888 + 88 + 8 + 8 + 8 = 1000.

Puzzle 7
150 miles.

I was travelling at 30mph at a rate of 20mpg, so I was using 1.5 gallons every hour for the driving itself.

I was also losing 0.5 gallon every hour. In total, I was using 2 gallons every hour.

Therefore to use all of the 10 gallons I started with, I travelled for 5 hours. 5 hours at 30mph is 150 miles.

Puzzle 8
The following is one answer, all other answers are a reflection or rotation of this.

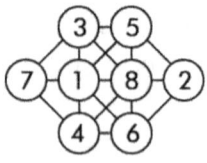

37.

Puzzle 9

1	4	2	2	1	2
4	3	1	3	4	3
2	1	4	2	1	2
1	2	2	3	3	1
4	1	3	1	2	1
3	1	4	3	4	2
2	1	1	1	1	3
3	4	2	3	2	2

Puzzle 10

Alan had a red boat and a green boat.

Brian had a green boat and a blue boat.

Charles had a yellow boat and a red boat.

Darren had a blue boat and a yellow boat.

Puzzle 11

148 inches.

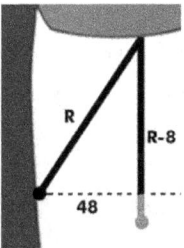

We can use Pythagoras' theorem if we draw an imaginary line across to create a right-angled triangle.

The hypotenuse is equal to the rope's length R. The bottom of the triangle is 48 inches. The vertical side is R - 8 (the difference between 20 inches and 12 inches).

Pythagoras' theorem tells us that:

$a2 + b2 = c2$

Where c is the hypotenuse.

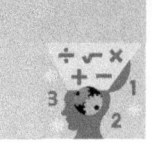

This gives us:
$482 + (R - 8)2 = R2$
$2304 + (R - 8)(R - 8) = R2$
$2304 + R2 - 16R + 64 = R2$
$2304 - 16R + 64 = 0$
$16R = 2368$
$R = 148$
As required.

Puzzle 12

Since the man at the back could not determine his own hat, this means that the front two men could not have been wearing black hats and that, therefore, there must be at least one red hat on the two front men.

Therefore the middle man must not be able to see a black hat, otherwise he would know he had a red one on.

Therefore the front man must be wearing a red hat - which finally he deduces. Interestingly, the other two can never determine their own hats.

Puzzle 13

24.

There were 12 pieces on the top layer with at least 2 sides with icing. The other three layers, each have 4 pieces that have 2 sides, with icing. A total of 24.

Puzzle 14

We have to be careful what we are adding together.

Originally, they paid £30, they each received back £1, they now have only paid £27. Of this £27, £25 went to the manager for the room and £2 went to the bellboy.

Puzzle 15

128.

There are 62 squares of size 1x1.
There are 41 squares of size 2x2.
There are 18 squares of size 3x3.
There are 6 squares of size 4x4.
There is 1 square of size 5x5.
A total of 62 + 41 + 18 + 6 + 1 = 128.

Puzzle 16

140 revolutions.

If we break each wheel into its prime factors, we get:

$168 = 2 \times 2 \times 2 \times 3 \times 7$
$49 = 7 \times 7$
$32 = 2 \times 2 \times 2 \times 2 \times 2$
$15 = 3 \times 5$

So

revolutions × 168
$2 \times 2 \times 2 \times 2 \times 2 \times 3 \times 5 \times 7 \times 7$
  revolutions × $2 \times 2 \times 2 \times 3 \times 7$
$2 \times 2 \times 2 \times 2 \times 2 \times 3 \times 5 \times 7 \times 7$
  revolutions
$2 \times 2 \times 5 \times 7$

revolutions

140

Which means revolutions = 140.

Puzzle 17

13.

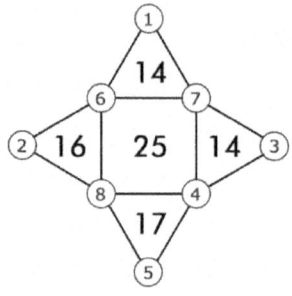

Puzzle 18

Puzzle 19

7÷27 of each coin was missing.

The original value of the three coins was 100 + 25 + 10 = 135, and the new value was 100. So 35÷135 of the original value has been removed and 35÷135 = 7÷27.

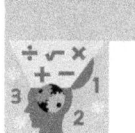

Puzzle 20

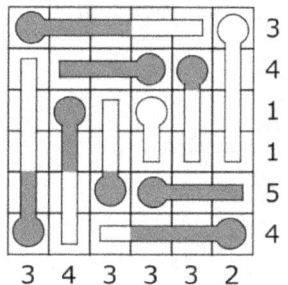

Puzzle 21

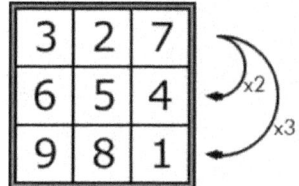

Puzzle 22

The distance must have been sixty miles.

If Sir Edwyn left at noon and rode 15 miles an hour, he would arrive at four o'clock - an hour too soon. If he rode 10 miles an hour, he would arrive at six o'clock - an hour too late. But if he went at 12 miles an hour, he would reach the castle of the wicked baron exactly at five o'clock - the time appointed.

Above is the answer given in the book, and below is a method of finding the answer.

If we call the distance to the castle, D and using the fact that Time = Distance ÷ Speed, we have:

Travelling at 15 mph:

$Time_1 = D \div 15$ (an hour too soon)

Travelling at 10 mph:
Time 2 = D ÷ 10   (an hour too late)
The time gap between these two times is 2 hours, therefore
Time 2 - Time1 = 2
D ÷ 10 - D ÷ 15 = 2
Multiply throughout by 30:
3D - 2D = 60
D = 60 miles.

Puzzle 23

3.
Checking that 3 works:

3   3   3   3
- - - + - = -
3   2   4   12

1 - 1.5 + 0.75 = 0.25

0.25 = 0.25, which confirms that 3 is correct.

To deduce the answer directly from the question, we can multiply throughout by 12,

*   *   *   *
- - - + - = -
*   2   4   12

to give:
12 - 6* + 3* = 1*
12 - 3* = 1*
12 = 4*
3 = *
As required.

Puzzle 24

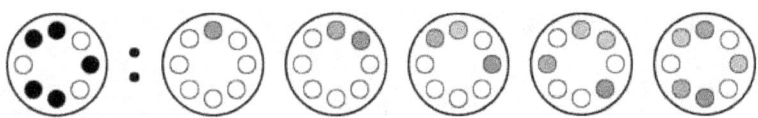

At each stage, a new dot starts at the top, and then goes either clockwise, or counter-clockwise.

Puzzle 25

Circle: 3.5.

Square: 3.1.

Triangle: 4.7.

Doughnut

The area of a circle is π × Radius 2.

The larger circle has diameter = 4, therefore the radius is 2, and the area is π × 22 = 4π.

The smaller circle has diameter = 2, therefore the radius is 1, and the area is π × 12 = π.

Therefore the shaded area is 4π - π = 3π ≈ 9.42.

Circle

The area of a circle is π × Radius2.

The circle with diameter 3.1 has a radius of 1.55 and an area of π × 1.552 = 7.55.

The circle with diameter 3.5 has a radius of 1.75 and an area of π × 1.752 = 9.62 (** closest match).

The circle with diameter 3.9 has a radius of 1.95 and an area of π × 1.952 = 11.95.

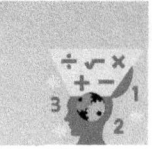

Square

The area of a square is Side × Side.

The square with side 3.1 has an area of 3.1 × 3.1 = 9.61 (** closest match).

The square with side 3.5 has an area of 3.5 × 3.5 = 12.25.

The square with side 3.9 has an area of 3.9 × 3.9 = 15.21.

Triangle

The area of a triangle is ½ × Base × Height. Using Pythagoras' theorem, it can be shown that the area of an equilateral triangle is Sqrt(3) × Base2 ÷ 4.

The triangle with side 3.9 has an area of Sqrt(3) × 3.9 × 3.9 ÷ 4 = 6.59.

The triangle with side 4.3 has an area of Sqrt(3) × 4.3 × 4.3 ÷ 4 = 8.01.

The triangle with side 4.7 has an area of Sqrt(3) × 4.7 × 4.7 ÷ 4 = 9.57 (** closest match).

Puzzle 26

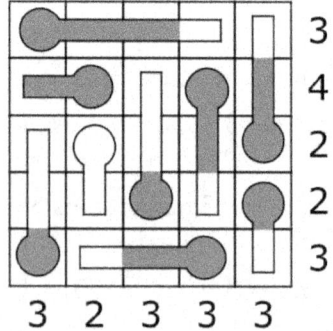

Puzzle 27

The age of Mamma must have been 29 years 2 months.

That of Papa, 35 years; and that of the child, Tommy, 5 years 10 months. Added together, these make 70 years. The father is six times the age of the son, and, after 23 years 4 months have elapsed, their united ages will amount to 140 years, and Tommy will be just half the age of his father.

The answer above is taken from the original book, here is another version of the answer:

If we call Tommy T, Mamma M and Papa P, we can see that:

"our three ages add up to exactly 70 years" leads to

$T + M + P = 70$ (1)

"Just six times as old as you" leads to

$P = 6 \times T$ (2)

In an unknown number of years (Y), "Shall I ever be half as old as you" leads to:

$P + Y = 2 \times (T + Y)$ (3)

and "our three ages will add up to exactly twice as much as to-day" leads to:

$(T + Y) + (M + Y) + (P + Y) = 140$

which can be written as

$T + M + P + 3Y = 140$ (4)

We can see from (4) and (1) that

$3Y = 70$

so

$Y = 70 \div 3$ (5)

Using (2) and (5) in (3), we have

$P + Y = 2 \times (T + Y)$

$6 \times T + 70 \div 3 = 2 \times (T + 70 \div 3)$

$4 \times T = 70 \div 3$

T = 70÷12 (6)
We can now use (6) in (2) to see that:
P = 6 × T
P = 6 × 70÷12
P = 70÷2
And using the values for T and P in (1) we have:
T + M + P = 70
70÷12 + M + 70÷2 = 70
Multiply throughout by 12 to give:
70 + 12 × M + 420 = 840
12 × M = 840 - 420 - 70
12 × M = 350
M = 350÷12
So: Tommy = 70÷12   = 5.83333 = 5 years 10 months.
Papa = 70÷2   = 35   = 35 years.
Mamma = 350÷12 = 29.1666 = 29 years 2 months.

Puzzle 28

2 hours.

In one hour, Fred eats 27 chocolates, Alice eats 12, and Kelly eats 21. A total of 60 chocolates. Therefore, 120 chocolates would take 120 ÷ 60 = 2 hours.

Puzzle 29

6	÷	2	=	3
+		×		
1	+	4	=	5
=		=		
7		8		

Puzzle 30

Panama.

Aliens landed in downtown Chicago last night. Most locals stepped outside to see the spaceship's massive wingspan. Amazingly, seven people failed to see the sight before them, as they took shelter from the great light that shone from upon high.

Puzzle 31

Either 2 or 3 depending on whether the initial two is halved fi rst.

"half of two" plus two

or

half of "two plus two"

The normal rules of BIDMAS/BODMAS do not apply to this question as this is not a mathematical expression, i.e., it is written as an English question, and not a well-formed Mathematics question.

Puzzle 32

Trip, Trio, Open, Pale and Palm.

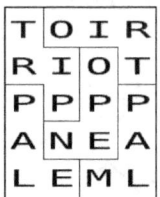

Puzzle 33

There is no possible way to complete the line, there will always be one edge left - or you have to cross an edge twice. This puzzle is the same as the famous 'Seven Bridges of Konigsberg' problem

first solved by Euler. In that problem, the task was to find a closed path that crossed each of the seven bridges of Konigsberg (now Kaliningrad, Russia) exactly once.

8.

Puzzle 34

+	4	—	2	+	2
2	+	2	-	2	+
-	1	+	2	-	4
2		1	+	1	-
+	1	-	2	+	3
3	+	3	-	4	+

Puzzle 35

C and E.

Puzzle 36

3211000.

Puzzle 37

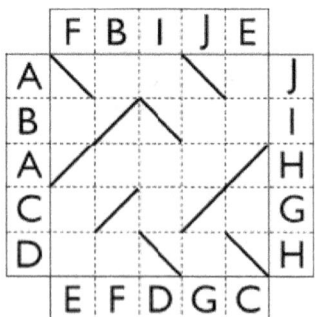

Puzzle 38

Place one letter from TEN HORSES into each of the nine stables.

Puzzle 39

120 miles.

On the fi rst day, I travelled 60 miles, leaving 60 miles. On day two, I travelled 20 miles, leaving 40 miles On day three, I travelled 30 miles, leaving 10 miles. Yesterday, I travelled 5 miles, leaving 5 miles.

Puzzle 40

```
      4 6
    5 9 1 9
  3 4 2 3 7 3
  5 8 6 9 8 2
    1 5 2 1
      6 7 8
      3 4 1
```

Puzzle 41

The way to arrange the sacks of fl our is as follows: 2, 78, 156, 39, 4. Here each pair when multiplied by its single neighbour

Answers

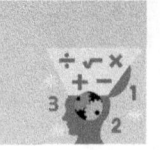

makes the number in the middle, and only five of the sacks need to be moved.

There are just three other ways in which they might have been arranged (4, 39, 156, 78, 2; or 3, 58, 174, 29, 6; or 6, 29, 174, 58, 3), but they all require the moving of seven sacks.

Brainteasers

Brainteaser 1
Turn on the first two switches and leave them on for 5 minutes. After 5 minutes, turn off the second switch, leaving the first switch on. Now go upstairs to the attic. The light that is on is connected to the first switch. A light that is off but has a bulb that is still warm to the touch is connected to the second switch. The light that is both off and cold to the touch is connected to the third switch, which was never turned on.

Brainteaser 2
The man waited for nightfall, and once it was dark, he exited through the door to the room made of magnifying glass.

Brainteaser 3
Fill the 5-gallon jug with water, pour it into the 3-gallon jug until the 3-gallon is full, leaving 2 gallons in the 5-gallon jug. Now pour out the water in the 3-gallon jug. Pour the 2 gallons of water (in the 5-gallon jug) into the empty 3-gallon jug. Fill the 5-gallon jug. You now have exactly 7 gallons!

Brainteaser 4
The statement that you and your friend each paid $14 for the meal is misleading and is, in fact, not accurate. The $14 actually

includes the meal and the tip. You each paid $12.50 for the meal (half of $25), $1.50 for a tip (half of $3) and each got back $1 in change. Add it all up and it comes to $15 each, for a total of $30.

Brainteaser 5

The numbers are organised by shapes!

In Row A, all the numbers have rounded shapes.

In Row C, all the numbers have linear shapes.

Row B is a mix of curves and lines.

Therefore, 16 goes to B, 14 goes to C and 38 goes to A.

Mind, Maths and Logic Quizzes

Ans.1. $2^6 - 63 = 1$ (In other words, $2 \times 2 \times 2 \times 2 \times 2 \times 2$, which equals $64 - 63 = 1$)

Ans.2. Take the chicken over first. Go back and bring the grain next, but instead of leaving the chicken with the grain, come back with the chicken. Leave the chicken on the first side and take the fox with you. Leave it on the other side with the grain. Finally, go back over and get the chicken and bring it over.

Ans.3. 3 socks. If the first sock is black, the second one could be black, in which case, you have a matching pair. If the second sock is white, the third sock will be either black and match the first sock, or white and match the second sock.

Ans.4. The numbers are in alphabetical order.

(eight, five, four, nine, one, seven, six, ten, three, two, zero)

Ans.5. Nothing. The 3 travellers paid a total of $27, making $25 for the hotel and $2 for the clerk. There is no missing $1.

Ans.6. The eye colour of the reader of this problem. The first sentence is the key: "You are the bus driver."

Ans.7. Neither, roosters don't lay eggs.

Ans.8. You get to figure this one out on your own. If you're having a hard time, here's a hint: There is a valid answer that doesn't require tricks like throwing the flashlight or shining it backwards or having some other means of moving the flashlight.

Answers

There's an assumption people often make that keeps you from solving this. Two members cross the bridge each time, but neither one of the two, who crossed need to return. Think about how that would be possible. If you're still stuck, use objects to simulate their movements. Use whatever you have laying around - pens, paper, erasers - and move them back and forth. Good luck!

Ans.9. By setting the snooze time to 9 minutes, the alarm clock only needs to watch the last digit of the time. So, if you hit snooze at 6.45, the alarm goes off again when the last digit equals to 4. They couldn't make it 10 minutes, otherwise the alarm would go off right away, or it would take more circuitry.

Ans.10. On a bookshelf, the first page of the first volume is on the "inside", so the bookworm eats only through the cover of the first volume, then 8 times 1000 pages of Volumes 2 - 9, then through the cover to the 1st page of Volume 10 for a total of 8,000 pages.

Note: The question asks how many pages, not how many sheets of paper.

Ans.11. The wise man tells them to switch camels.

Ans.12. Since the bridge is 4 kilometres long, the halfway point would be 2 kilometres. The 18-wheeler would have used much more than 30g of fuel to drive 2 kilometres.

Ans.13. It was during the day

Ans.14. It's the cabin of a plane and the plane crashed.

Ans.15. To rotate the handle on the mug, so that she can comfortably remove it.

Ans.16. Beulah and Craig were hurricanes.

Ans.17.

1. Flip both hourglasses over and drop the egg into the water.

2. When the 4-minute timer runs out, flip it over (4 minutes elapsed, 3 remaining on the 7-minute timer).

3. When the 7-minute timer runs out, flip it over. (7 minutes elapsed, 1 remaining in the 4-minute timer)

4. When the 4-minute timer runs out, flip the 7-minute timer over. (8 minutes elapsed. 6 minutes remained in the 7-minute timer, but flipping it over leaves one minute's worth of sand on top. When it runs out exactly, nine minutes will have elapsed.

Ans.18. Four canaries and three cages.

If you put one canary in each cage, you have an extra bird without a cage. However, if you put two canaries in each cage, then you have two canaries in the first cage, two canaries in the second cage and an extra cage.

Ans.19. The next number in the sequence is 1113213211, because the rule for creating the next number is to simply describe the previous number. The first number is 1, or 1 (one) 1, so you get 11. To describe 11, you have two 1's, or 21. Now you have one 2 and one 1, so the next number is 1211. The solution is to simply continue describing the previous number using only numbers.

Ans.20. Four daughters and three sons.

Ans.21. Tom

Ans.22. They are triplets.

Ans.23. None. The boat is floating on the water, so as the tide rises, so does the ladder.

Ans.24. Light the first fuse on both ends and the second fuse at only one end. When the first fuse burns out you know 30 minutes have passed. Light the other end of the second fuse and when it burns out, 45 minutes have passed.

Ans.25.
Fill the 3-gallon bucket.
Pour the 3 gallons of water into the 5-gallon bucket.
Fill the 3-gallon bucket again.

Fill up the 5-gallon bucket with the 3-gallon bucket, leaving you with 1 gallon left in the 3-gallon bucket.

Empty out the 5-gallon bucket.

Pour the remaining 1 gallon of water from the 3-gallon bucket into the 5-gallon bucket.

Fill the 3-gallon bucket.

Pour the 3 gallons of water from the 3-gallon bucket into the 5-gallon bucket leaving you with 4 gallons of water in the 5-gallon bucket.

Alternate solution:

Fill up the 5-gallon bucket.
Pour it into the 3-gallon bucket, leaving 2-gallons.
Empty out the 3-gallon bucket.
Pour the 2-gallons in the 5-gallon bucket into the 3-gallon bucket
Fill up the 5-gallon bucket and pour it into the 3-gallon bucket until it's full, leaving 4-gallons in the 5-gallon bucket.

Ans.26. This one took a while, but I figured it out. You can find the answer here.

Ans.27. She walked on the bridge towards Switzerland for 3 minutes and just as the guard was about to come out, she turned around walking back to Germany. The guard saw her and asked for her pass but she didn't have one and was sent back (or what the guard thought was back) to Switzerland. In her case, it was the very country she wanted to go to.

Ans.28. He made a perfect copy of a counterfeit bill.

Ans.29. You will hang me.

Ans.30. The trick is that the word dead represents a number in the hexadecimal. That number in base 10, plus one to include yourself, is: 57005 + 1 = 57006.

Ans.31. The man in the picture is his son. Since he doesn't have any brothers or sisters, the statement my father's son is himself.

A shortened version would be this man's father is myself, so he is the father of the man in the picture.

Ans.32. The surgeon was his mother.

Ans.33. Asked the princess to touch his hand.

Ans.34. They were facing each other. As to why his companion was smiling, the world may never know.

Ans.35. Get off the merry-go-round.

Ans.36. Take x coins, flip all of them and put them in one pile. The rest of the coins form the second pile.

Ans.37. 3 cuts. Cut each link in one chain. Separate them, and use the links to join the ends of the 3 intact chains.

Ans.38. The one labelled both. Since you know it's labelled incorrectly, it must have all black marbles or all white marbles. After you determine what it contains, you can identify the other two boxes by the process of elimination.

Ans.39. The water level remains unchanged because the ice cube displaces its own weight. If you're not convinced, read Archimedes' Principle, which states that any floating object displaces its own weight of fluid.

Ans.40. First weigh three coins against three others. If the weights are equal, weigh the remaining two against each other. The heavier one is the counterfeit. If one of the groups of three is heavier, weigh two of those coins against each other. If one is heavier, it's the counterfeit. If they're equal weight, the third coin is the counterfeit.

Ans.41. 3, 3, and 8. The only groups of 3 factors of 72 to have non-unique sums are 2, 6, 6 and 3, 3, 8 (with a sum of 14). The rest have unique sums:

2 + 2 + 18 = 22
2 + 3 + 12 = 18
2 + 4 + 9 = 15
3 + 4 + 6 = 13

The house number alone would have identified any of these groups. Since more information was required, we know the sum left the answer unknown. The presence of a single oldest child eliminates 2,6,6, leaving 3,3,8.

Ans.42. Ask either guard what door the other guard would say is the exit, then choose the opposite door.

If you ask the guard who always tells the truth, he knows the other guard would lie, so he'll point you to the door leading to death. If you ask the guard who always lies, he knows the other guard would truthfully show you the exit, so he'll lie and point you to the door leading to death.

An alternate solution is to ask a guard what they would answer if you were to ask them which door was the exit, then choose that door. The truthful guard will point to the correct exit, but the lying guard will too. Here's why. If you asked him what door was the exit, he would normally lie and point to the death door, but you asked him what he would say if you asked what door was the exit, and in order to lie to that question, he will point you to the exit.

Ans.43. Halfway. After that it will be running out of the forest.

Ans.44. 240. To get the number, multiply the previous number in the series by its position. 48 is in the 5th position, so 48 × 5 = 240

Ans.45. Place 1 white marble in one bowl, and place the rest of the marbles in the other bowl (49 whites, and 50 blacks).

This way you begin with a 50/50 chance of choosing the bowl with one white marble and living. Even if you choose the other bowl, you still have an almost 50% chance of picking one of the 49 white marbles. There are no guarantees in life, but this is your best bet at surviving.

Ans.46. To get the next number, multiply the previous number in the series by itself plus one: $n * (n+1)$. For example, to get 6, multiply 2 * 2+1. To get 42 multiply 6 * 6+1.

Thus, 1806 * 1807 = 3263442

Ans.47. f(n,m) = (n + m) * n
e.g. f(2,3) = (2 + 3) * 2 = 10
Hence, f(9,7) = (9 + 7) * 9 = 144

Ans.48. The syllables in the numbers from 1 to 20

Ans.49.

80 from store 1 = $4

1 from store 2 = $1

19 from store 3 = $95

Ans.50. It's the numbers 0 through 10 in alphabetical order.

Ans.51. The missing numbers are 4 and 9. The list is sorted alphabetically by the English spelling of the numbers, so four belongs after fi ve and nine comes after fourteen.

Ans.52. 2178

Ans.53. First: $57.14, Second: $28.57, Third: $14.29

Ans.54. The maid. Mail isn't delivered on Sunday

Ans.55. The letter e is the most common letter in the English language, yet it never appears in the entire paragraph.

Ans.56. The third room, since the lions would be dead.

Ans.57. Yesterday, today and tomorrow.

Ans.58. Pour the water from the 2nd glass into the 5th glass.

Ans.59. A=1, B=3, C=9 and D=17

1lb = A

2lbs + A = B

3lbs = C

4lbs = A + B

5lbs + A + B = C

6lbs + B = C

etc.

Ans.60. f(x,y,z) = 10000*(x*y) + 100*(x*z) + transpose_digits(x*y + y*z)

transpose_digits() just swaps the digits

Ans.61. Pressing these digits in sequence will produce HELLO WORLD on a cell phone (for an SMS text message)

Ans.62. The men are widowers and married each other's daughter.

Ans.63. "new door" can be rearranged into "one word"

Ans.64. There are three men: A grandfather, a father (the grandfather's son) and the father's son.

Ans.65. All words with a repeated letter are allowed. Green glass door, apple and ball.

Ans.66. T - they all rhyme.

Ans.67. 2 minutes (The back of the train would be at the beginning of the tunnel after 1 minute, and would leave the end of the tunnel at the 2-minute mark.

Ans.68. Water (if the teaser worked, you guessed milk)

Ans.69. A comb. Rhonda likes words with silent letters, like her name.

Ans.70. 34 times. These 17 instances will be visible twice in a 24 hour period.
1:11 2:22 3:33 4:44 5:55 10:00 11:10 11:11 11:12 11:13 11:14 11:15 11:16 11:17 11:18 11:19 12:22

Ans.71. The dog can jump over his doghouse.

Ans.72. None, they all flew away because of the noise.

Ans.73. Two of the passengers were Siamese twins.

Ans.74. A baseball game.

Ans.75. Because his night watchman was sleeping on the job.

Ans.76. One thousand (or one hundred and one, depending on how you pronounce it.

Ans.77. He hung the hat up on his gun.

Ans.78. 5 cats. The same five could keep catching 5 mice every 5 minutes for 100 minutes.

Ans.79. Look in the mirror, then at the wall and back at the mirror to see what you saw. Use the saw to cut the table in half and join the two halves to make a whole. Put the "hole" on the wall and climb out. (I know, it's lame)

Ans.80. There is no staircase, it's a ranch.

Ans.81. It was during the daytime.

Ans.82. They all have homonyms: currant, buy, due, phase, lone, eight

Ans.83. 5 4 5 + 5 = 550

Add a diagonal line on the top left of the first plus sign to convert + into a 4. You could also put a slash through the equal sign to make (not equal) but that's not as cool.

Ans.84.
Tom took the apple
Jim was telling the truth
Hank was telling the truth
Tom was lying
Don was lying
Eddie was telling the truth
(3 telling the truth and 2 lying)

Ans.85. 142857 (The first 6 digits of 1/7)
2 × 142857 = 285714
3 × 142857 = 428571
4 × 142857 = 571428
5 × 142857 = 714285
6 × 142857 = 857142

Ans.86. 24 hours in a day
26 letters of the alphabet

7 days of the week

9 lives of a cat

12 signs of the Zodiac

88 piano keys

Ans.87. Fish. The gh is pronounced as in tough, the o as in women and the ti as in nation. Ghoti is a constructed word to illustrate irregularities in English spelling.

Ans.88. I understand you undertake to undermine my undertaking.

Ans.89. Persisting

Ans.90. Turn it upside down and look at it in a mirror.

Ans.91. 675.

The next number in the sequence is n squared minus m or $f(n,m) = n^2 - m$

$f(6,9) = 6^2 - 9 = 27$

$f(9,27) = 9^2 - 27 = 54$

$f(27,54) = 27^2 - 54 = 675$

$f(54,675) = 54^2 - 675 = 2241$

Ans.92. Two 50lb boys cross, one comes back.

100lb boy crosses, other 50lb boy returns

Both 50lb boys cross.

Ans.93. It's winter and the water is frozen.

Ans.94. A. If Anne is married, she's looking at George, who is unmarried. If Anne is unmarried, Jack is looking at her.

Ans.95. 91. To get the number in the fourth column, you add the numbers in column 1 and 2, then multiply by the number in column 2. $f(n,m) = (n + m) * m$

For example, $f(2,3) = (2 + 3) * 3 = 15$. Thus, $f(6,7) = (6 + 7) * 7 = 91$

Ans.96. 2 and 4

Ans.97. 4 days

Day 1: up to 10, down to 4

Day 2: up to 14, down to 8

Day 3: up to 18, down to 12

Day 4: up to 22 (20 really) and done

Ans.98. They weren't playing each other.

Ans.99. Put 7 pigs in the first three pens and arrange the fourth to contain the other three.

Ans.100. The man was a checkout clerk at the grocery store. The list was for items to get at a lingerie store.

Ans.101. 1st - Jimmy, red car

2nd - Kevin, blue car

3rd - Larry, yellow car

4th - Mike, green car

5th - Nader, orange car

Ans.102. His car door

Ans.103. Yes. The President was Ulysses S. Grant, who died in 1885 and whose face has been on the $50 bill since 1913. He saw the President on the bills before he made the exchange.

Ans.104. 194

Ans.105. It allows them to be rolled around easily and prevents the cover from falling into the hole.

Ans.106. 5 owls and 5 wolves, (not 6 owls because 2 of the eyes and legs are yours).

2 * owls + 2 * wolves = 20 eyes

2 * owls + 4 * wolves = 30 legs

owls + wolves = 10 eyes   owls = 10 - wolves

owls + 2 * wolves = 15   10 - wolves + 2 * wolves = 15   wolves = 5

owls + 5 = 10   owls = 5

Ans.107. When putting gloves on, then removing them.

Ans.108. Eat (8) fl ush (plus) to (2) my nose (minus) tree (3) times (times) for (4) they buy dead by (divided by) too (2).

There are two answers depending on whether you calculate as you read or calculate the entire solution at the end.

$8 + 2 = 10, - 3 = 7, \times 4 = 28, / 2 = $ **14**

or

$8 + 2 - 3 \times 4 / 2 = 10 - 6 = $ **4**

Ans.109. A $50 bill, a $5 bill and 4 $2 bills.

Ans.110. 4,100. If you got 5,000 you're not alone. 96% of test subjects get the wrong answer.

Ans.111. There are six. Most people skip the word 'of' and only count three.

Ans.112. $3 * (5 - 6) + 2 * 54 - 5$

$-3 + 108 - 5$

$105 - 5 = 100$

Ans.113. The taxi driver is not in his cab, he's out for a run. The house he went through was his own because he had fi nished running.

Ans.114. Weigh four against four. If they're equal, weigh three of them against three you haven't weighed. If they balance too, weigh the last remaining egg against any of the others to see if it is lighter or heavier. If the three suspects are heavier, weigh one of them against another and the one that goes down is it. If they balance the remaining suspect is heavy. Use the same process if they're lighter. If the initial four vs four don't balance, weigh two heavy eggs and a light egg against one heavy egg, one light one and a known normal egg. If they balance weigh the remaining two light eggs against each other. If they balance the unweighed heavy egg is the odd one out. If the side with two heavy eggs goes down, weigh them against each other. If they balance, it is

the light egg on the other side. If the other side goes down, it is either because of one heavy egg on that side or because the one light egg on the other side is lighter than the rest. Weigh one of them against a known normal egg to determine which is true.

Ans.115. 3 ½.

If you break up the numbers into groups of 4, a,b,c,d, then $2 \times |a - d| = |b - c|$.

9 2 4 8 $2 \times |9 - 8| = |2 - 4|$, or $2 \times 1 = 2$
4 3 7 6 $2 \times |4 - 6| = |3 - 7|$, or $2 \times 2 = 4$, so
n 3 2 3 $2 \times |3 ½ - 3| = |3 - 2|$, or $2 \times ½ = 1$;

Ans.116. 3:36pm. For every 60 minutes of real time, the clock moves 50 minutes. Put another way, 60/50 = 1.2 real minutes per slow-clock minute. In order for the clock to show 3:00pm, 180 of its slow minutes have to pass. 1.2 * 180 clock minutes = 216 real minutes or 3 hours and 36 minutes.

Ans.117. A football player who was tackled

Ans.118. A + 1 = 2A, so A = 1.
A + 1 = B - 1, so B = 3.

Ans.119. Luke, because there's no power (it's during a blackout).

Ans.120. Potatoes (Pot + 8 Os)

Ans.121. 91 - 67 = 24 or
(9 - 6) × (7 + 1) = 3 × 8 = 24

Ans.122. Glass.

Ans.123. The contestant should switch doors, which doubles the chance of winning the car. Initially there is a 2/3 chance of picking a goat, but once the other goat is revealed, switching to the remaining door gives the contestant a better chance of winning the car. This is known as the Monty Hall Problem and can be very unintuitive.

Ans.124. Yes, because a plane's wheels roll freely and have no affect on the movement of the plane(unlike a car). The propellor

or jet engine makes the plane move and the plane will be able to take off normally. If you don't believe me, here's the proof.

Ans.125. An ambulance doesn't pour water.

Ans.126. Working together they can stock a shelf at a rate of 1/20 + 1/30 (or 5/60) per minute. They'll finish in 12 minutes.

Ans.127. Door numbers at $3 each.

Brain Drainers

Ans 1. Second Place. If you pass the person in second, you take second place, and they become third.

Ans 2. They all do.

Ans 3. You don't bury the SURVIVORS!

Ans 4. I can predict the score BEFORE it begins. Well, the score before any football game is always zero to zero!

Ans 5. First take the hen across. Leave the hen. Go back and get the fox. Take the fox to the other side. Leave the fox there, but take the hen with you back to get the corn. Leave the hen and take the corn to the other side. Drop the corn off with the fox, then go back to get the hen. Bring the hen to the other side. All three make it fully intact!

Ans 6. Many will get 5000. But the actual answer is 4100!

Ans 7. 6. 3 for each team.

Ans 8. A fifty-cent piece, and a nickel. I said 'one is not a nickel', but the other one is!

Ans 9. Jimmy. "JIMMY'S MOTHER had 4 children!"

Ans 10. Whatever colour your hair is! Remember, you are the bus driver!

Ans 11. Mt. Everest. It was still the highest in the world – it just hadn't been discovered yet!

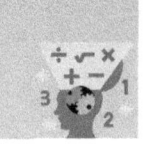

Ans 12. White. The only place you can hike 3 miles south, then east for 3 miles, then north for 3 miles and end up back at your starting point is the North Pole. There are only polar bears in the north pole, and they are white!

Ans 13. The man is a dwarf. He can't reach the upper elevator buttons, but he can ask people to push them for him. He can also push them with his umbrella.

Ans 14. A highly depressed man with a flair for the dramatic decided to kill himself. So he built a large wooden box with one door. Strung some rope through the top and made a noose. He then got a 3x3 block of ice, and put it below the rope. After nailing, the door shut from the inside, he stood on the block of ice, put the noose around his neck and jumped off. Hours later the police found him hanging with only a puddle of water and a hammer in the room.

Ans 15. A baseball game is going on. The base-runner sees the catcher waiting at home plate with the ball, so decides to stay at the third base to avoid being tagged out.

Ans 16. Three. In the worst case, the first two socks you take out will consist of one black sock and one white sock. The next sock you take out is guaranteed to match one or the other.

Ans 17. This is possible, and there are 2 ways to do it: Solution 1: Fill the 3-cup bucket, pour it into the 5-cup bucket. Fill the 3-cup bucket again, and pour it into the 5-cup bucket until the 5-cup bucket is full. That will leave exactly 1 cup of sugar in the 3-cup bucket. Dump out the 5-cup bucket, and dump the 1-cup from the 3-cup bucket into the empty 5-cup bucket. This leaves 1-cup in the 5-cup bucket. Now fill the 3-cup bucket again and add it to the 5-cup bucket. Now you have exactly 4-cups of sugar in the 5-cup bucket! Solution 2: Fill the 5-cup bucket. Pour it into the 3-cup bucket. This leaves 2-cups in the 5-cup bucket.

Dump out the 3-cup bucket. Now pour the 2-cups from the 5-cup bucket into the 3-cup bucket. Refill the 5-cup. Now pour the 5-cup into the 3-cup until the 3-cup is full. That will leave exactly 4-cups in the 5-cup bucket!

Ans 18. Two half-full barrels are dumped into one of the empty barrels. Two more half-full barrels are dumped into another one of the empty barrels. This results in nine full barrels, three half-full barrels, and nine empty barrels. Each son gets three full barrels, one half-full barrel, and three empty barrels.

Ans 19. The rules of the race were that the owner of the camel that crosses the finish line last wins the fortune. The wise man simply told them to switch camels.

Ans 20. Fill the 5-gallon jug, pour it into the 3-gallon jug until the 3-gallon jug is full, leaving 2 gallons in the 5-gallon jug. Now pour the 3-gallon jug out. Pour the remaining 2 gallons from the 5-gallon into the empty 3-gallon jug. Now fill the 5-gallon jug from the faucet. You now have exactly 7 gallons.

Ans 21. You ask either man the following question: "If I asked the other guy which door has the money, what would he say?", then choose the opposite door. Work it out: If you ask the question to the liar, he will lie about the 'correct' answer, so you must choose the opposite door. If you ask the truth teller, he will tell the truth about the lie, so you can choose the opposite door as well.

Ans 22. The accounting method is wrong. The $2 is actually a part of the $27, and shouldn't be added to it as stated in the problem.

Ans 23. The back man can see the hats worn by the two men in front of him. So, if both of those hats were white, he would know that the hat he wore was black. But, since he doesn't answer, he must see at least one black hat ahead of him. After it becomes apparent to the middle man that the back man can't figure out

what he's wearing, he knows that there is at least one black hat worn by himself and the front man. Knowing this, if the middle man saw a white hat in front of him, he'd know that his own hat was black, and could answer the question correctly. But, since he doesn't answer, he must see a black hat on the front man. After it becomes apparent to the front man that neither of the men behind him can answer the question, he realises the middle man saw a black hat in front of him. So he says, correctly, "My hat is black."

Ans 24. His son.

Ans 25. A river!

Ans 26. The catcher and the umpire.

Ans 27. A sponge.

Ans 28. 1 paisa.

Math Riddles

Riddle-1
Because it is too gross (2 × 144 - two gross).

Riddle-2
Both weigh the same.

Riddle-3
They both have 4 quarters.

Riddle-4
A leg.

Riddle-5
When there are two of them.

Riddle-6
Only one, after that the basket is not empty.

Riddle-7
A half dollar.

Riddle-8
24 cents.

Riddle-9
8.

Riddle-10
At a yard sale.

Riddle-11
None - they are copycats.

Riddle-12
You have three apples.

Riddle-13
A bed.

Riddle-14
Once; after that it is no longer 30 (Don't try this in a test!)

Riddle-15
$0.0125

Riddle-16
20.

Riddle-17
One pound is twice of half pound.

Riddle-18
The letter 'e'.

Riddle-19
Cut XII into two halves horizontally. You get VII on the top half.

Riddle-20
Your fingers.

Riddle-21
They need to be changed.

Riddle-22
10, 5 on each side.

Riddle-23
Your age.

Riddle-24
Wow, have I got problems!

Riddle-25
Otherwise it would be a foot.

Logic Games and Riddles

1. Riddle
The key to this math riddle is realising that the one place must be zero.
888 +88 +8 +8 +8 =1,000

2. Two Fathers and Two Sons Riddle
One of the 'fathers' is also a grandfather. Therefore, the other father is both a son and a father to the grandson.

In other words, the one father is both a son and a father.

3. Digit Frequency
Explanations for both riddles

The digits 0 through 9 all follow the same pattern. There is exactly 1 occurrence of each digit for every ten numbers.

For instance, the digit 2 appears once between 10 and 19, at 12. And 2 appears once between, 30 and 39 at 32.

However, each of the digits, 1 through 9 also appear in other numbers in the tens and hundreds place.

Again, let's look at 2 which appears in 20,21,22, 23, etc. as well as 200, 201, 202, 203.

So to figure out how to answer the first riddle, you had to see what distinguishes the number 1? Only that we are including 1,000

which would be the first '1' in a new series of ten! In other words, the digit 1 only has a single extra occurrence (301 occurrences) compared to 2 or 3 or 9 which each have exactly 300 occurrences.

The reason that zero has the least (BY FAR at only 192 occurrences) is because zero does not have any equivalents to 22, 33, 44, 222, 3333, etc.

4. Three Guys at a Hotel Riddle

There are many ways of explaining/thinking about this truly brain bending riddle! It all boils down to the fact that the lawyers's math is incorrect. They did NOT spend $9 • 3 + $2.

They spent exactly $27 dollars. $25 for the room and $2 for the tip. Remember they got exactly $3, in total back.

Another way to think about the answer to this riddle is to just pretend that the bellhop refunded $3 to the lawyers (rather than giving them $5 and receiving $2 back). If the lawyers get $3 back and each takes $1, they spent exactly $27 dollars.

5. Foreign Country Riddle

The answer is 4

$$\frac{1}{2} \circ 5 = 3$$

$$\frac{1}{3}\left(\frac{1}{2} \circ 5 = 3\right)\frac{1}{3}$$

$$\frac{1}{6} \circ 5 = 1$$

$$2\left(\frac{1}{6} \circ 5 = 1\right)2$$

$$\frac{2}{6} \circ 5 = 2 \to \frac{1}{3} \circ 5 = 2$$

$$2\left(\frac{1}{3} \circ 5 = 2\right)2$$

$$\frac{1}{3} \circ 10 = 4$$

6. The Merchant

11 cartons total

7 large boxes (7 * 8 = 56 boxes)

4 small boxes (4 10 = 40 boxes)

11 total cartons and 96 boxes

7. Crossing the River

The key to solving this riddle is realising that you have to take the rabbit over first and the switch the fox with the rabbit. See step 2.

Step 1) Take the rabbit to the other side

Shore	Other Side
Carrots	
Fox	Rabbit

Step 2) Go back and get the Fox and switch it with the Rabbit **The key here is that the carrots and the rabbit are not being left alone.

Shore	Other Side
Carrots	
Rabbit	
(Not left alone)	Fox

Step 3) Take the carrots across.

Shore	Other Side
Rabbit	Fox
Carrots	

Step 4) Go back and get the rabbit

Shore	Other Side
Rabbit	
Fox	
Carrots	

8. Three Brothers on a Farm
Every farmer's part is 1/3(45+75) = 40 sacks.
Charlie paid $1400 for 40 sacks, then 1 sack costs $1400/40 = $35/sack.
Adam got $35*(45-40) =35*5 = $175.
Ben got $35*(75-40) =35*35 = $1225.
Answer: Ben $1225, Adam $175

SELF IMPROVEMENT

128 pp • ₹ 150   168 pp • ₹ 195   179 pp • ₹ 96   228 pp • ₹135   121 pp • ₹ 120   120 pp • ₹ 72
(Also available in Tamil ₹ 96)

143 pp • ₹ 68   112 pp • ₹ 108   130 pp • ₹ 96   136 pp • ₹ 96   128 pp • ₹ 96   176 pp • ₹ 120

128 pp • ₹ 80   108 pp • ₹ 120   142 pp • ₹ 88   175 pp • ₹ 120   123 pp • ₹ 96   165 pp • ₹ 120

STRESS

 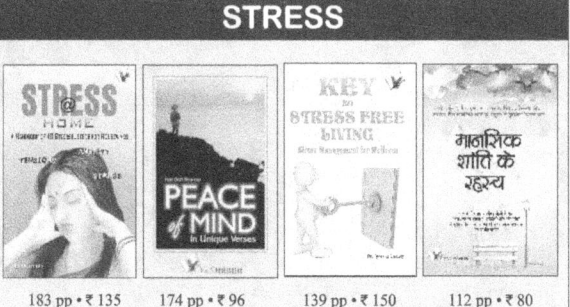 

260 pp • ₹ 175   183 pp • ₹ 135   174 pp • ₹ 96   139 pp • ₹ 150   112 pp • ₹ 80   124 pp • ₹ 96

All books available at www.vspublishers.com

PERSONALITY DEVELOPMENT

120 pp • ₹ 96   156 pp • ₹ 96   120 pp • ₹ 108   151 pp • ₹ 96   128 pp • ₹ 60   128 pp • ₹ 60

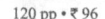

120 pp • ₹ 88   134 pp • ₹ 110   142 pp • ₹ 88   112 pp • ₹ 96   160 pp • ₹ 96   175 pp • ₹ 110

CAREER & BUSINESS

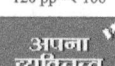   

190 pp • ₹ 135   223 pp • ₹ 150   96 pp • ₹ 120   124 pp • ₹ 150   224 pp • ₹ 150   256 pp • ₹ 175
(also available in Hindi ₹ 135)

RELIGION

207 pp • ₹ 195 (HB)   268 pp • ₹ 249 (HB)   242 pp • ₹ 96   186 pp • ₹ 499 (HB • Colour)   220 pp • ₹ 225
120 pp • ₹ 80   296 pp • ₹ 175   152 pp • ₹ 135

All books available at www.vspublishers.com

ASTROLOGY / PALMISTRY / VAASTU / HYPNOTISM / OCCULT

BHAGAVAD GITA

 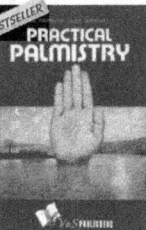   

136 pp • ₹ 120   386 pp • ₹ 135   252 pp • ₹ 120   142 pp • ₹ 96   484 pp • ₹ 165

 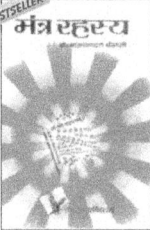   

266 pp • ₹ 108   380 pp • ₹ 120   191 pp • ₹ 96   144 pp • ₹ 88   75 pp • ₹ 60

122 pp • ₹ 80   800 pp • ₹ 320 (HB)   122 pp • ₹ 96   180 pp • ₹ 80   110 pp • ₹ 50

FICTION   HUMOUR & SATIRE

256 pp • ₹ 195   128 pp • ₹ 175   136 pp • ₹ 175   114 pp • ₹ 60   144 pp • ₹ 48   124 pp • ₹ 48   120 pp • ₹ 80

256 pp • ₹ 195   209 pp • ₹ 195   136 pp • ₹ 135   114 pp • ₹ 48   144 pp • ₹ 48   144 pp • ₹ 48   108 pp • ₹ 60

All books available at www.vspublishers.com

STUDENT DEVELOPMENT

QUOTATIONS

122 pp • ₹ 150
(also available in Hindi ₹ 120)
(Free CD)

64 pp • ₹ 120
(colour)

142 pp • ₹ 110

143 pp • ₹ 80
(also available in hindi)

164 pp • ₹ 120

132 pp • ₹ 80

257 pp • ₹ 120

230 pp • ₹ 88

205 pp • ₹ 96

152 pp • ₹ 96

133 pp • ₹ 150

132 pp • ₹ 80

144 pp • ₹ 96

QUIZ / BRAIN TEASERS / PUZZLES

256 pp • ₹ 200

152 pp • ₹ 110

131 pp • ₹ 175   148 pp • ₹ 120

187 pp • ₹ 125

192 pp • ₹ 96

112 pp • ₹ 48

127 pp • ₹ 120
(also available in Hindi ₹ 120)

256 pp • ₹ 120

85 pp • ₹ 60

90 pp • ₹ 60

All books available at www.vspublishers.com

POPULAR SCIENCE

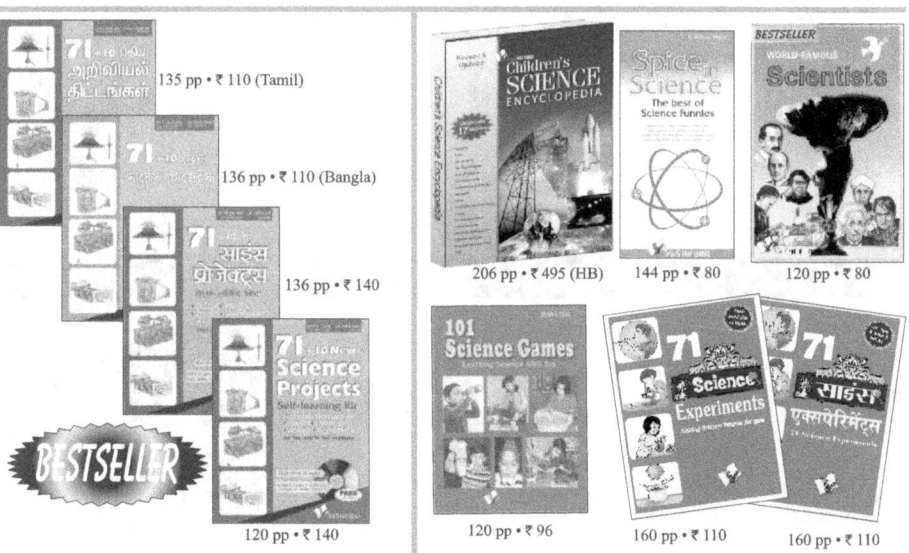

All books available at www.vspublishers.com

GENERAL HEALTH

163 pp • ₹ 96   180 pp • ₹ 96   198 pp • ₹ 96   ₹ 449 • A set of 4 Books   176 pp • ₹ 175

ALTERNATIVE THERAPIES | AYURVEDA

104 pp • ₹ 96   144 pp • ₹ 96   112 pp • ₹ 80   310 pp • ₹ 135   175 pp • ₹ 75

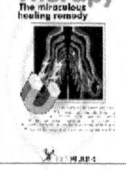  

125 pp • ₹ 108   135 pp • ₹ 108   119 pp • ₹ 96   220 pp • ₹ 175   150 pp • ₹ 96

DISEASES & COMMON AILMENTS

 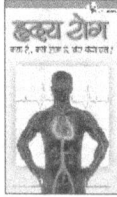   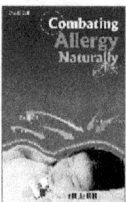 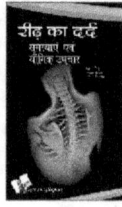 

136 pp • ₹ 135   156 pp • ₹ 96   120 pp • ₹ 96   132 pp • ₹ 135   119 pp • ₹ 96   64 pp • ₹ 60   200 pp • ₹ 108

All books available at www.vspublishers.com

YOGA & MEDITATION

104 pp • ₹ 96

144 pp • ₹ 96

93 pp • ₹ 80

BEAUTY CARE

136 pp • ₹150   120 pp • ₹ 125

DIET & NUTRITION

160 pp • ₹ 96

130 pp • ₹ 120

165 pp • ₹ 96

173 pp • ₹ 125

115 pp • ₹ 96

BODY FITNESS

245 pp • ₹ 120

204 pp • ₹ 150

156 pp • ₹ 95

209 pp • ₹ 108

HOUSEKEEPING

256 pp • ₹ 175

192 pp • ₹ 150

144 pp • ₹ 96

144 pp • ₹ 96

292 pp • ₹ 150

All books available at www.vspublishers.com

FUN / FACTS / MYSTERY / MAGIC

128 pp • ₹ 100

501 ASTONISHING FACTS
124 pp • ₹ 80
(also available in Hindi ₹ 60)

111 pp • ₹ 72

MAGIC for CHILDREN

120 pp • ₹ 80
(also available in Hindi ₹ 72)

CHILDREN STORIES

Interesting Stories on PROVERBS
98 pp • ₹ 96

कहावतों की कहानियाँ

120 pp • ₹ 96

जादू का जादू
112 pp • ₹ 72

GREATEST CRAFTS & PROJECTS for CHILDREN

112 pp • ₹ 100

World Famous UNSOLVED MYSTERIES

136 pp • ₹ 100
(also available in Hindi ₹ 72)

136 pp • ₹ 72

कहानियाँ
88 pp • ₹ 80

पंचतंत्र की कथाएँ
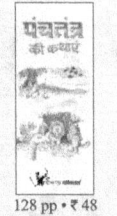
128 pp • ₹ 48

RELATIONSHIPS & SEX

All you wanted to know about...
144 pp • ₹ 96

सेक्स के 111 सवाल
120 pp • ₹ 80

पति-पत्नी सम्बन्ध सदा मधुर रहें
192 pp • ₹ 96

नारी
190 pp • ₹ 96

PARENTING

बच्चों की प्रतिभा कैसे उभारें
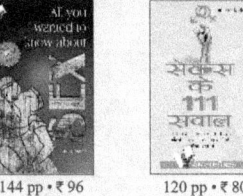
191 pp • ₹ 72

How to shape your Kids Better

124 pp • ₹ 96

32 pp • ₹ 48(colour)

152 pp • ₹ 96

Parent's Gift for a Child

83 pp • ₹ 50

Raising a Daughter

136 pp • ₹ 120

माँ
132 pp • ₹ 96

Pregnancy with Yoga & Dietetics

129 pp • ₹ 150

COOKERY

भारतीय व्यंजन

80 pp • ₹ 72

Modern Cookery Book
176 pp • ₹ 150

आधुनिक पाककला
176 pp • ₹ 150

101 Curries

136 pp • ₹ 80

101 पकवान खाना खजाना

125 pp • ₹ 96

100 FAT-FREE

117 pp • ₹ 96

COOKING MADE EASY

102 pp • ₹ 80

All books available at www.vspublishers.com

www.ingramcontent.com/pod-product-compliance
Lightning Source LLC
Chambersburg PA
CBHW070337230426
43663CB00011B/2348